WHAT DO YOU DO WHEN YOUR NICKNAME'S JOB?

Jessie,
God bless
you as you walk
with the Lord on
your journey.
Jane Sneed

WHAT DO YOU DO WHEN YOUR NICKNAME'S JOB?

you gotta have faith

JANE SNEED

TATE PUBLISHING & *Enterprises*

Published by Tate Publishing & Enterprises, LLC
127 E. Trade Center Terrace | Mustang, Oklahoma 73064 USA
1.888.361.9473 | www.tatepublishing.com

Tate Publishing is committed to excellence in the publishing industry. The company reflects the philosophy established by the founders, based on Psalm 68:11,
"The Lord gave the word and great was the company of those who published it."

Cover design by Kellie Southerland
Interior design by Joey Garrett

Published in the United States of America

ISBN: 978-1-61663-102-4
1. Religion / Christian Life / Personal Growth
2. Biography & Autobiography / Personal Memoirs
10.06.15

TABLE OF CONTENTS

INTRODUCTION

It has been almost three years since I started the journey of writing my book. It began approximately four months before my husband passed away. The specific night it started was when I arrived home and realized that my husband, Jeff, had been in the hospital for six straight months. He had been very ill, and unless God provided a miracle the inevitable was going to happen. Throughout our twenty-three years of marriage, Jeff and I experienced so many things, and because of them I sit here and reflect on how God has carried us through each one. I also want to share what God has brought me through since burying Jeff and, dealing with the feelings of loss and depression that I have endured for the past two and a half years.

My desire is to share how God's wonder and mercy has gotten me to this point of reflection. I told my friend just hours ago that however God wants to use me is how I want to be used. The Lord has put it on my heart over and over again to write a book and become a speaker for His kingdom. This may not sound crazy to you but I am a high school math teacher—not an English teacher. I seem to be way out of my league here. God definitely works in mysterious ways.

Every time I read a Christian book by someone, I always want to know what has gotten them to this place. What has God done in their life to make them able to understand things that people struggle with? Sometimes I am so blessed by their words that I don't always have to know. In my own book, message, or whatever you would call something that is a first attempt for a forty-seven-year-old woman, I feel that God wants me to share specifically how I have walked through some of the trials in my life. I don't want you to think that I, in any way, walked perfectly or piously through any of these challenges. I can definitely say that through it all God used each experience to bring me to a closer walk with Him.

It has been hard to come to the point of sharing things openly. Things that are embarrassing, scary, stupid, and just plain painful, but again I want to obey my Lord. If anyone can be helped by my life, then I want to be used. As I mentioned before, we were married twenty-three years before Jeff died. Throughout our marriage we had several challenges. Jeff had unemployment issues which caused terrible financial problems. Other challenges we faced were addictions to alcohol, drugs, gambling, and pornography. Verbal abuse from my spouse was frequent. We have also been through a tubal pregnancy, impotency for the last eleven years of our marriage, health issues of my own, the deaths of my father and brother-in-law, and the tragedy of dear friends being taken far too quickly from this earth.

I hate writing this down because it makes me face everything again. It also makes me say negative things about someone I loved and who I have watched suffer and slowly die over the past few years. I am definitely not blaming all of our difficulties on my husband. This is not a husband-bashing book, but unless I am honest I can't help others. As I share all of the things listed above, and others that will come later in the book, I want it understood that God has seen us through everything. As I look back on each bump, or should I say mountain in the road, we have been blessed. We have two beautiful children, a daughter twenty-one and a son fifteen. All babies are miracles, but believe me it is amazing that they are here and healthy. Most importantly, they have made decisions to accept Jesus as their Savior, putting Him first in their lives. Our girl has graduated with a Veterinary Technician degree, our son is a freshman in high school. Both of them have been through so much pain and confusion. We are all walking our own separate paths, seeming to deal with the loss in different ways, but the Lord is the constant in what each of us is going through and He will help us survive this tragedy for His glory.

If you have been through any of these issues, I urge you to read this book and let the Lord's word bless and encourage you. I cannot imagine any better way to glorify Him than to let others know how much you can live through when you lean on the Lord. Believe me, I also have been in places in my life that I swore if another person quoted, "God won't give you more than you can handle, or all things work together for good for those who love the Lord, or I can do all things through Christ who strengthens me," I would scream at them to shut up. I am now truly understanding what it means to really lean on the Lord and to have "Job-like" faith.

I remember sitting in a Women of Faith Conference and listening to Barbara Johnson speak about all of the tragedy she had encountered with her sons. She made me laugh until I was crying while she shared. I want to be able to laugh, cry, and share just like those fine ladies who have blessed my life. My prayer tonight at 1:30 a.m. is that God will use what I have to share to bless even one person or save even one marriage or help one obese person find self-worth through the Lord. So "what do you do, when your nickname's Job?" ... you gotta have faith!

> Oh Lord, please help me to say and share the right things. There have been so many situations in my life and I want you to help me choose the right ones, share the right scriptures and remember to put you first in this endeavor. Lord, I pray this will be blessed by you and will glorify your name. Thank you so much for using me. In Jesus, precious name, Amen.

FAILURE WITH FLAB

> Will you rely on him for his great strength?
> Will you leave your heavy work to him?
>
> Job 39:11

It amazes me how everyone thinks a chubby baby and toddler is adorable and then at the age of four if they haven't trimmed down then they are disgusting and just plain fat. As I look back on my childhood, teen years, and adult life the one thing that has been a constant failure is my flab.

I have been on every diet from Weight Watchers, Weigh Down, liquid diets, L.A. Weight Loss (which wouldn't work because I live in St. Louis) and numerous exercising binges. At one point or two I actually lost some weight; the most significant amount was about eighty pounds until recently. I have dealt with many things that I needed to overcome with the Lord's help, but this weight thing is the most difficult. What always has made me crazy is I am not an obese woman because I lay around all day eating bon bons, or the kind that has a secret closet with ding dongs in it. I am just a normal person who loves good food, and of course my top three choices would be bread, potatoes and chocolate. This couldn't be the problem, right?

My momma has always said that it is a shame that other sins can be hidden but when you are overweight that is just right out there for everyone to see. An alcoholic can look great at a dinner party, a gambler doesn't wear a sign, a verbally abusive person knows when to behave, but if you weigh 300 pounds you can't appear to be perfect. I really take offense to people who look at me with condescending eyes and opinions when they don't even know me. I work hard, I have a great personality and I am much greater than the worth that some have labeled me. Over the past ten years, I have tried to analyze, dissect, and reason why this is just something I haven't been able to be successful at. With the advice of thin relatives and friends who say continuously just do it, it's not that hard or just put your mind to it. All I can say is it is hard and it is something I face daily each time I look in the mirror.

I was saved at the age of ten and was raised in a wonderful Christian home with godly parents who took us to church every time the doors were open. I am the fourth generation of my mom's family to attend there. My dad was a deacon and my mom was blessed with the gift of being a pianist at our church. (I often compare my life with Chonda Pierce who wrote Second Row Piano Side because I was, "First Row Piano Side." I would love to be half as funny as Chonda.) They took me, my older brother and two older sisters to church;

sharing God's wonderful word with us continually. They are definitely a testament that even godly parents can have struggles: a son who is an addicted gambler, children's divorces, and day to day attacks from the evil one that sabotage anything that brings God glory.

I am the baby of the family, and was very involved in church, the choir, and Sunday school. At the age of seventeen, I flirted enormously with my future husband. I need to interject that I have had the awful challenge of being overweight my entire life, not just in my adult years. I was the heavy, jolly girl who everyone loves to be with but no guy would really want to date. Well, my sweet husband looked past my fat and saw the inside of me, my heart, and my desires. I like to believe he was complimenting me when he said, "I was the prettiest fat woman he had ever seen." Of course, he didn't say that for the four years we were dating, or he probably wouldn't have been my husband, but since the wedding that was said often. When we started dating I was about 180 pounds. When we got married I was about 210 pounds. After ten years of marriage, I was about 280 pounds. Then after two pregnancies, I stayed around 300 pounds. During the last six months of Jeff's life, I put on about sixty more pounds due to the hospital, fast food, and yes, stress. My struggle with my weight is the one thing God and I are still dealing with, and definitely the one thing that I must get victory over for Him to be able to fully use me.

Now I do realize that there are those of you out there that maybe aren't as obese as me, but I know that all of us look at ourselves so critically that I am sure you can relate these feelings to something you feel is not pretty or has destroyed your own self-esteem. If you have trouble with an aspect of yourself always remember that God made you who you are. You are not a mistake. You are here for a reason. Don't you ever forget that each one of us was knit together in our mother's womb. I plead with you to daily lay down your struggle with yourself and give it to our Almighty God so you will have victory and peace throughout the day. As Luke 9:23 states, we need to take up our cross daily and with the Lord's help we can give it to Him and let it go each and every day.

I am constantly asking myself how God can use me when I am such a failure with His temple. I have been convicted that God is going to use me no matter what my faults are, because He sees my heart and knows my desires. I have been making excuses for years. Why can't I do this? God no longer wants me to wait until I have it all together before I share. No matter how closely we walk with the Lord we all are still going to have weaknesses and shortcomings. And believe me, it is not my only one, I have several, but this is foremost in my heart.

My daughter, for the first time, is looking for a job and is scared and insecure about going out there and putting herself in a position to be hired or not wanted. I know it sounds crazy but I am watching her with the apprehension and nervousness of doing something so new that it scares her to death, and I see my life with the same problem. I have never been anything but overweight and I am scared to death to be thin. My personality which has gotten me many friends and jobs through the years is who I am, and even for a huge person I have positive self-esteem. Would that be the same if I lost a whole person? My fat has been a comfort, a friend, a protector and a horrible excuse my entire life. I know who my comfort and my friend should be and it is definitely not food. With the Lord's help I will lose this weight because at this time in my life it is not about appearance but it is about survival. My health has gotten so bad that I can hardly move, and I know that this is a victory the Lord wants me to win if I will only let Him lead the way.

I have repeated I can do all things through Christ who strengthens me several times over the last few days. I am trying to be smart and healthy about my food choices. I cannot get on some quick fix scheme to lose weight; I have to make it my way of life. God is my refuge and strength and has gotten me through so many things that I know if I lay it at His feet daily; I can do this. I am tired of making excuses, blaming my childhood, blaming my stress, blaming my medicine. I need to face the facts: I am weak but Jesus is strong and He can carry me through anything.

Let me explain what I mean by blaming my childhood. My brother was six years older than me, and was in great shape and very athletic. I would eat one twinkie in the box; he would eat six and tell mom that I didn't need one twinkie at all. He would verbally abuse me and call me names so it was not only at school but at home that I was treated this way. I have forgiven my brother through much prayer over the years. Even now as an adult he will say things to encourage me to lose weight for my health, but now does it in a slightly kinder, mature way. I don't know if obesity is passed down, or if it is cultivated behaviorally as a child. I do know that how you look at food is molded in the early years and can damage you the rest of your life. Now, I am not blaming my mom for being a wonderful cook, and I am not blaming my brother for teasing his little sister about being fat but I am just trying to figure it out for myself as I am writing it to you.

During my preteen and teen years, it was a buffer to not do anything wrong physically with a boy. A way to make sure they wouldn't like me in that way. All the guys loved to hang out with me and tell me everything about other girls because I was so easy to talk to and fun to be with. I did enjoy those years, but deep down I had several secret crushes that never went anywhere because those boys only enjoyed my flirting, my sense of humor and my ability to be fun. I look back on it now and know how much I just wanted to feel pretty enough for just one of them to want me as a girlfriend, and not a friend that was a girl. During my junior and senior years of high school, people at school did look beyond my size, and I had friends. But my world was the youth group at my church where I always felt secure in my identity, well, as much as a teenage girl can feel. In college, I was already seriously dating Jeff. I know that I could have dated others by that age because as people mature they look at the true person and not just the outside.

You might want more specifics about me. I have

blue eyes with hardly any lashes and dishwater blonde hair (but in the summer it gets lighter), and I am five feet six inches tall. I am very colorful in my outfits—I don't hide in a corner because of my size. I love my job, and amazingly enough, high school students are the most open to like me even though I am big. Their kindness and acceptance reflects how I treat them, and I know that God has given me this blessing of great relationships with teenagers to help me feel accepted for who I am and not for how I look. I have taught in a few different public high schools which I consider my own little mission field, I try daily to show my students Jesus' love and they all know my beliefs and respect them. If I was at a job where I felt no support for who I was, I would not be able to be as positive with my size as God has helped me to be.

A few stories were repeated throughout my life as I was growing up that might help you get to know me better. I was a little over a year old when I was innocently crawling through our kitchen, heading straight for the open door to our basement when my mom, who was doing dishes, turned and saw me. In her attempt, at least that is what she always told me, to stop me from hurting myself she leaped to grab me, falling on her face, and instead of saving me she pushed me out over the stairs to our basement. While she lay helpless at the top, watching me free fall through the air she screamed, and my dad, who was outside cutting grass, came running in to the basement and hung himself on the clothesline trying to get to me before I crashed on the concrete floor. I was rushed to the hospital because

I was bleeding around my mouth. Miraculously, I only needed three stitches in my lower lip. That night I was laughing and playing with my toys, dad had an ice pack on his neck, and mom was hysterical for what she had done to her baby.

When I was born, my brother wanted a boy so badly that he sat on the front steps, pouting because now he had three sisters. So I was a huge disappointment for him from day one. Maybe that is why he teased me relentlessly. My parents had three children two years apart and then six years later my mom thought she had the flu, but, oh no, I was not the flu I was the "accident." Now, my mom tries to say I was the icing on their three cupcakes, but for years I was teased about being a surprise, an accident, and yes, an unexpected blessing.

My parents were not wealthy at all and struggled to make ends meet. After the first three kids were born my mom had a beautiful portrait done of her children. Beautiful outfits, beautiful children, two, four and six. They all still had their baby teeth and they really were beautiful. That picture hung over our mantle my entire life. Yes it is still there, and it makes it look like for all who come in that the Hartin's had three children. Through the years mom would randomly put a picture of me on the mantle to make me feel better, but even though I have teased her over the years about this and said it is no big deal, I think it may be part of my identity problem. What am I saying? I don't have an identity problem, I am a child of the King, and He knows who I am—but I will say that this picture thing has probably made me obsessed with pictures. I am constantly taking them and my children are constantly posing for their maniac momma. I have pictures of students on every wall of my classroom. I am so sentimental about memories and people I love that pictures are very important to me. I, unlike a lot of people who are overweight, let people take pictures of me. I want to be remembered and I want to remember those who have touched my life. I do Creative Memories and love what joy it brings me to share those albums with my family and my children. God has blessed me so much and I like people to see what those blessings are.

Between the ages of 40 to 47 I began to not have the energy to care about myself. I was so focused on everything else in my life that to worry about me was just too much. But what God has helped me realize over the past month is that I really don't have an option now. If I want to have any possibility of being here and live a normal life, then I have got to get thinner. I am on high blood pressure medicine, thyroid medicine, a water pill, a pill to stop kidney stones, an antidepressant and 100 units of an insulin mix twice a day. This is not a healthy woman. I have been in the hospital several times with pneumonia, kidney stones, and dehydration, and these visits don't include all of the complications I had with my pregnancies. Why don't we, as overweight people, feel special enough to take care of ourselves?

I have said over and over in my lifetime, I don't care if I am fat. If people don't want to love me for who I am then who needs them. But God has shown me that people do love me for who I am. They love me enough that they want me to be healthy. As obese people, we do care that people stare, or that little kids say to their parents, "Hey, look how fat they are." It has gotten to the point where I have to constantly be thinking if I will fit in a restaurant booth, if the table moves so I can squeeze in, or if I will fit through the turnstile at a baseball game. I try to press on, to go to the beach because I love the sun, and to do things with my kids even though I can hardly move. It has been about a week since I started writing and so far God is helping me reinforce that through Him all things are possible.

I need to interject here that I was athletic growing up and actually can still shoot a pretty good shot in basketball. That's what makes this even sadder: I can't do the things I have always enjoyed. I used to play basketball, softball and volleyball. I have been a coach for cheerleading and volleyball. My knees are messed up, not only from the weight, but because when I played volleyball we didn't use knee pads and I would always dive on the gym floor to save the ball. On the beach if my son wants to play any type of catch or paddle ball I can give him maybe fifteen minutes and then I am done for the day. I want to change that and be able to physically enjoy my life before it is way too late. I pray each day that there is still time for this change.

Already with nine days of trying to do all things through Christ who strengthens me I have failed for about two of them. I can't believe how emotionally drawn I am to food. I get so angry when I eat something I shouldn't, and then because I am upset I blow it some more. I know what has changed during those two days, I wasn't spending time in God's word, and I wasn't spending time with the Lord during those days like I normally do.

We had a huge storm go through the county and city. My home was without electricity for four days, so while I stayed at my sister's I was not on task with my diet. What I have to finally realize is that I will not be perfect for the next two years or the rest of my life, but when I do eat something I shouldn't, I need to let it go. I need to get over it and start fresh immediately. I always would wait for Monday morning or the day after a holiday or a birthday party to start a diet over and still with no success because every day would bring its own temptation. Again, with the excuses and again with not facing the fact, I must change my habits and I must be strong even in the face of temptation.

> God, please forgive me where I fail you. Please help me in this endeavor to lose weight, Lord. My husband is gone and my children need a healthy strong parent to be with them. I cannot do it without you. Guide my paths to make the right choices in everything, but especially with the challenges of food. Thank you for bringing me to this place of brokenness. I love you, Jesus. Amen.

It has been about three weeks since I started watching what I ate and I have blown the last seven days. The devil always throws some type of craziness into the mix to make me lose my focus. After we lost our electricity for four days, I had to throw out about two hundred dollars worth of healthy food. Then we found out about a student of mine who was killed in a car accident and my husband had his last birthday and, and, and ... I just keep making excuses. I am, again, picking myself up and pleading with the Lord to forgive me and help me be stronger. There have been other times where I have gotten a great start then I would end up in the hospital, someone else would go in the hospital, my mom would have a stroke, or there was a vacation planned. Again, I have got to quit making excuses and stand strong in the midst of turmoil. I am being honest and letting you see how human I am because all of us go through the same things, same frustrations and same difficulties. We all need to just remember where our strength lies. Along with that, the number one thing you need to truly believe is that with God's help you can slay your Goliath, just like David.

After yet another week of failure I went on my vacation. So naturally food is fun and food is best when eaten out while you are on vacation. I, of course, will get serious again when I go back to work at a high school with snack food available to me all day long. Again I know that I can do all things through Christ who strengthens me, but I know that my failure is not because of the Lord. I have not given it all to Him and over and over again I take it back and fail on my own strength.

During a doctor visit for a complete physical I found out that having a baby wasn't the most difficult thing to do, I would have to say that it is trying to go potty in a one inch diameter cup when you weigh 360 pounds. Oh, my gosh. I almost had a heart attack trying. My life is such that the doctor doesn't even yell at me anymore for my weight. He will say that I need to lose but he will not say much because he knows that I am in some nerve-racking situations, and he doesn't want me to break down in the office. When I had been there four months before my mother had just had her stroke and this time I mentioned that I just witnessed an eighteen year old student buried on Monday. Being already maxed out on antidepressants, he suggested a psychiatrist. I don't like him to think that is what I need. I tell him again and again that the Lord will take care of me, but he doesn't know what else to do to help me. I am not sleeping well at all. They think that if I have someone outside of all the situations to talk to that I would feel better and then lose weight. I know that a psychiatrist will not help me in the way I need it, but as my doctor said, maybe it would be nice to share with someone who isn't sick of listening. Some of my friends don't know what to do anymore so they just quit calling. My health is so fragile right now that I must get my act together and fast. There is no quick fix and there is no Oprah coming around the corner to give me my own nutritional chef for a year. I have the most important ingredient to what my life needs, a perfect Savior.

> Lord, please forgive me again for not controlling what I put in my mouth. God, give me the strength and courage to continue to try. Help all those people out there with the same problem I have to give our appetites to you daily and pray before each

meal for self-control. Thank you for your patience with me. In Jesus' name I pray. Amen.

I have not written now for about three months. After getting back from summer vacation; starting school and getting my daughter settled in at a different college, Jeff passed away, Wednesday, September 7, 2006. Experiencing all of that will be in a different chapter but I bring it up in this one to explain how the Lord blessed me with my weight problem. Watching Jeff suffer so much and just seeing his little body slowly die has convinced me more than ever I have got to get healthy. For the major part of the book Jeff was alive, but now he is gone and I want to share the new struggles I am having with you.

A little over a month after burying my 44 year old husband I had to go to the doctor again. They kept a real close eye on me because of all of my health issues. While I was there the doctor shared with me my blood results and they were the worst ones I had ever had. I believe out of approximately ten things they checked that eight of mine were bad. My blood sugar over the past few years was running between 250 and 350 and I could not seem to get it under control. I shared about Jeff's passing and started crying with my doctor, telling him that I was so scared and so tired of being unhealthy. He decided to refer me to a diabetic specialist who also had a special diet program for people who really needed help. I met with this doctor and after talking with him we both decided that I needed something drastic to help me with this weight problem.

I started an all liquid diet on October 24, 2006 and did not chew anything except sugar free gum for almost a year. After being on the diet 25 days I lost 29 pounds. After just nine days I was taken off my insulin all together and my blood sugars were running between 80 and 120. I felt amazing. I survived Thanksgiving with my family and did not cheat once. I felt the presence of the Lord with me and had strength and a will power I have never felt before. I realize this was a drastic choice and will not be right for everyone, but it worked for me. I planned on losing 200 pounds, drinking only liquids until that happened, and then joining Weight Watcher's when I reached my goal weight.

I thought I had finally figured out why other diets had not worked for me: I am lazy with food. I don't want to weigh, measure, count calories, or make choices. This supplement was the only choice I had four to five times a day and the results were amazing. Again, this is not for everyone, but I encourage each of you to find the diet that fits your needs.

We have all been on diets when we were very disciplined and made good choices only to go weigh in and gain a half of a pound; so, of course, we get discouraged. Then the next week we cheat a few times and lose four pounds. Where is the logic in that? Remember I teach Math so I like things that make sense and I couldn't stand the inconsistency of the scale. When I went to the doctor every two weeks, being monitored very closely, I knew I would lose. I just didn't know how much. At six months without food I had lost 115 pounds. God is magnificent and the joy He provided me through losing all of the weight was overwhelming. Realize that you are special and deserve to be healthy. You have a right to care about yourself. I believe most overweight people are the most unselfish caregivers to others but can't care for themselves. You are worthy. Christ suffered and died for you. You are beautiful and unique. Believe in yourself and just watch the miracles that happen.

The Lord has also blessed me with a very dear friend who helped me work out three to five times a week just to get me moving again. We were taking it very slow but I knew God put all of these things in my life to give me the support and guidance I needed. I spent so many years taking care of Jeff that I had gotten to a point where I could have become that 500 pound person who didn't get out of bed anymore. The thought of my children not having either parent made me realize I had to do something. I felt so much better being healthier and being able to do even more things to glorify God. I need to be involved in my church and do the things God has asked me to do instead of lying around feeling sorry for myself. If you have reached a desperate place in your life talk to a doctor, check out the options and let God use whatever He can to give you the life He so desperately wants you to have. To be full in His love and power instead of food is such an amazing feeling. I pray for the strength to continue and to finally overcome this awful addiction.

The truly scary part was when I would start eating again. I would have to change my whole approach to eating, and my whole idea of what food is for. Food is to sustain your body, not to give comfort, celebration or encouragement. During this diet I have changed. I know I have been delivered from this addiction with the obsession of food. The Lord can deliver each and every one of us from anything if we will let Him. Just like when the people were delivered out of Egypt by Moses. It took them several years to get where they were going because of sin and rebellion, just like it took me several years to be delivered from this eating disorder. The Lord continued to guide and convict them, as He did me, to reach their destination. When they did they were blessed beyond belief. Today, we are still rebelling, sinning, and going in circles. I would like to challenge you to quit struggling and pray for deliverance. God is waiting with open arms. He wants to be in a relationship with us that is personal and all encompassing. Won't you let Him be your all in all? I guarantee that when you get to this place in your walk with the Lord you will truly understand how much He loves you. There is no better feeling then to consistently walk with the Savior and rest in His arms.

> Oh, my sweet Savior, thank you so much for helping me through this stressful and depressing time of burying my husband. You have given me this unbelievable source of strength to daily lean on you for my spiritual food and for the successes I have already received in this endeavor. Thank you for bringing me to this place, and Lord help me to continue to lean on you. In your precious son's name. Amen.

FREEDOM FROM FAT FINALLY ... OOPS, MAYBE NOT

> Because of the Lord's great love we are not consumed, for his compassion's never fail.
>
> Lamentations 3:22 NIV

I had lost 183 pounds since burying my husband on September 11, 2006. It was August 4, 2007, and with the Lord's help I had done this in less than a year. I was feeling so many different things at this amazing accomplishment but my number one feeling was fear. Remember that I have always been overweight, that the only clothes I ever bought, even as a child, were from the chubby sections in Sears, and that I never got to shop in a normal store. I went from fear to being thinner, to shock that I was wearing a size 12 and then joy that I was so much healthier.

My sister said that I really weighed about 130 pounds

and I was carrying around 50 pounds of hanging flab. However, I did think that the flab was a good theory because I was wearing size 12 and 14's and I know when I weighed 180 pounds before when I was 17 years old that I could never have gotten in a size twelve.

I definitely spoke too soon about my freedom from fat. On December 14th I had been eating again for about 5 weeks and I still had not faced my demons of overeating. I stopped the diet when I got to 183 pounds and in those 5 weeks I put on 15 pounds. I realized through that month that I never dealt with my eating disorder. Now, I actually ate healthy things, but once I started I did not control how much I consumed. I honestly wished that I could never eat again. When an alcoholic quits drinking he can never touch a drink again, when a gambler needs to refrain from gambling he can stop going to places to gamble, but a food-aholic has to eat food to survive so to abstain from it is definitely impossible.I was told when I started eating again it would be very difficult to give up the food again. It was March 10, 2008 and I had bounced up and down with my weight over and over in the past few months. I had gained fifty pounds in those five months. It is unbelievable how fast I have always been able to lose and gain weight–even so much as fifteen pounds in just one day in either direction and I know this being a yo-yo with my body is so unhealthy. I have got to give this overwhelming mess to the Lord.

Approximately a year ago, I joined Celebrate Recovery at my church, and I am now finally facing my food addiction. The Lord has helped me see through this uncontrollable intake of food; that my addiction is just as bad as anyone else's. In my introduction of this book I stated that I did not hoard food or sneak it but now I am doing that. My body was in starvation mode for a year and when I started eating I couldn't control my desire to eat. I can't control anything but with God's help I am going to conquer this sin.

The following is what God laid on my heart to read at my first Celebrate Recovery meeting, to confess in the big group what was happening to me:

"It is February of 2008 and I am unbelievably back where I was in March of last year with my weight. Would someone please just glue my mouth shut? I have never, even at 360 pounds, had this obsession with food. It is all I think about and I don't eat out of hunger, but I just eat everything in sight. It is like I am pregnant and anything sounds good, at any time, in any combination. I feel like I have lost my mind and the food monster has taken over. I have gone from 174 pounds in August of 2007, my lowest weight ever, and am now 226 pounds. I think I was 174 pounds for about 10 seconds. I have got to stop this madness and that is just what it is."

"I have tried everything I can possibly think of: Weight Watchers, journaling, reading the Bible whenever I think of food and trying to do the liquid all over again. My doctor was right: once you eat, it is a nightmare getting back on just liquid. Shame on those people that told me I looked anorexic at 174 pounds, and that I had to eat because now I am out of control and I can't seem to stop the spiral. All of us food-aholics know that we start diets on Monday mornings or the first day of a new month or the day after a special event. I have tried all those things and again nothing—not one bit of success. Please God hear my cry, and help me this day, February 7, 2008, to only obsess about you and how much I love you and not food.

"The food I am choosing isn't brownies, fudge, pizza or fried chicken; it is healthy food, but just 5000 calories a day. I have now somehow given myself permission to go out of control if I deem the food healthy. Twenty granola bars in a two hour period, salad with cheese, chicken, croutons but fat free dressing, fat free potato chips, fat free anything but ten of them at the same time. Remember in the first chapter I said I didn't eat food in a closet but now I have become that person. Hiding food and buying food and eating it before I get home, and I am just overcome with this insane woman who can't control herself.

"The looks you get from people that care but don't know what to do, the sympathy stares, the "man she is stupid" stares, the pity stares and the, "I knew she couldn't stay thin" stares are all driving me crazy. With God's help all things are possible and I will get a handle on this today! I am now praying about fasting for a few days to cleanse my mind and body and just pray about my life and everything in it. I have made it for about an hour and a half. I seem to be fine until about 4:00 in the afternoon and then from 7 to 10 p.m. I am crazed. I don't know if it is loneliness, depression, self-destruction or what but God can conquer all of those things if I just let Him. Lately, it seems when I need to cry out to Him I turn in the other direction. The devil is not going to win, I am not going to give up and I will be healthy for my kids and do God's will in my life.

"I want to speak on success in losing weight to fellow women and I don't think I can do that if I was successful for six hours. God is in control of my life, my job, my family, and my mind and I have got to let Him have each of these things. The one thing that I have a choice about is what I put in my mouth, and I am failing myself and everyone else. My job is a mess right now, my family is changing and it is scary. My mind is overwhelmed with worry and stress but I have gotten through far greater things, and my Lord has seen me through each of them. The Bible says to look at the past things God has done to remind us of what He can do in the future. I need to remember what the Lord has allowed me to accomplish and just lean on Him through all of this.

"I have to do this. I gave all of my fat clothes away to charities and I have nothing to wear. Thin clothes don't stretch like my fat clothes did. When you are buying 26's they stretch with 30 pounds in either direction but a size 12 doesn't have much leeway and I am busting out of them. I don't like feeling bloated. I don't like feeling ugly. I don't like feeling like a failure. I don't like feeling stupid. I don't like feeling out of control. So why do we let our addictions overtake us?

"I am trying to rationalize what is going on and why God is allowing this to happen. Don't you like how I worded that like God is the problem? We can justify anything, can't we? I am wondering if He is doing this to show me what a true addiction is like. To realize how the alcoholic feels, the drug addict feels and the gambler when they have to have their next drink, fix or run at the tables. I don't think I ever felt like I was addicted to food but just made poor choices, and fat runs in my family, and made excuses all the time but now I can truly say I have an addiction and it is overtaking my life and I don't like it.

"The shame and confusion that addicts walk around with; I thought I understood before but now I truly can say that I have been there. My anger at Jeff for never controlling his addictions to pornography, drugs, cigarettes and alcohol is over. I have to forgive him to let myself free of the anger and hate I felt for what he did to himself and to our family. He was a weak man but, who am I to judge because I am just as weak and no matter what I try in my own strength I cannot accomplish it but in God's strength all things are possible. Everyone who is breathing has problems, hurts and hang-ups and even though I hate the fact that when I fall everyone can see what I have done by the size of my body, doesn't make my addiction anymore unforgiveable than the ones who are out there and are hiding what they are doing. If you have stumbled and fallen in your weakness, please allow God to help you get back up. First, we have to forgive ourselves and then ask God to forgive us and then take each moment at a time with our Almighty Father.

"I have three different types of people in my life right now: the group that just smiles and says nothing (my sweet sister Suzanne can't stand what is going on but her love is so abundant that's all I feel), the group that says, "hey Jane how's the exercise going" and the group—well actually, just one person—my sister, Pam who is honest with me and wants to kill me for gaining all this weight. They all mean well and they all are worried and concerned, but just like before at 363 pounds I had to make the decision to lose the weight and no one else could make it for me, so regardless of what anyone says or does I have to be the one to repent and turn toward the Lord and have Him help me through this addiction that I have let get out of control. Please take a moment to pray for all the people in this world who are struggling with something, any addiction that has overcome their mind and heart, and ask God to give them strength.

"If I keep saying things like, 'I still have lost 140 pounds so I am good,' then I am going to get right back to where I was and in record time. I can gain 15 pounds in one day and not even blink. My daughter, bless her heart, has that same ability. Maybe we could make that a television show, instead of the biggest loser how about the biggest gainer? How fast can a contestant gain weight, and they win a million dollars. I would definitely be a contestant. Seriously, don't you want to kill those thin people who say, 'Oh, I am such a mess. I have gained 5 pounds in the last 10 years'? What is that? Are they serious? I can gain five pounds looking at someone eating.

"I deserve the weight I have gained, I have been totally out of control, and I have made those unwise choices, so I am the only one to blame. I can't blame my life, my job, my children, or anything else. It is my fault. I have a huge problem and being on the liquid diet I never faced my demon of food or why I do it. I ignored it for a year and lost weight, but no wonder I cried at my first meal and didn't want it to happen because I knew I wasn't ready to face food and make good choices.

"Why do we let our addictions run our lives? We know they are bad, we know they bring heartache and confusion, we know that we feel better when we are free from them and we still make poor choices. Lord, I am so sorry for being so weak. Lord, please help me stand firm with you as my Rock and stand strong with you as my Strength. Hold me in your arms Lord so I don't feel so lonely, discouraged and confused because I want to share our awesome power with others and experience the joy that only you can give. Thank you, Jesus, for loving all of us with our scars and our weaknesses and continuing to always love us through it all."

I ended my confession with these two scriptures and felt a huge weight lifted off of my shoulders: Lamentations 3:55–58: "I called on your name, O Lord, from the depths of the pit. You heard my plea: Do not close your ears to my cry for relief. You came near when I called you and you said, 'Do not fear.' O Lord, you took up my cares; you redeemed my life," and Lamentations 3:22–23: "Because of the Lord's great love we are not consumed, for his compassion's never fail. They are new every morning; great is your faithfulness." Although that was a good step to make,

I still struggle daily with my food habits. I am going to Celebrate Recovery weekly and am learning how to give the Lord my addiction minute by minute. The people there are all so kind and accept me as I am because everyone there is dealing with something and they understand what I am feeling. There is no judging or hating but only Christ's unconditional love.

> Lord, I am begging you to forgive me of where I fall short, forgive me if I have hurt anyone and help me Lord to walk with you. I need you Lord more than I ever have, I am dealing with an addiction so powerful and all I want is to be addicted to you, your word and your will for my life. The devil is not going to win, my Lord will be victorious. Amen.

I feel so discouraged but with God I will be victorious.

I feel so stupid but knowing the Lord makes me brilliant.

I feel so overwhelmed but with God all things are possible.

I feel so embarrassed but God will protect me from evil doers.

I feel so useless but with God I will be used.

Please, Lord, help all of us who are controlled by things. Help us give our addictions to you and to let them go daily at your feet. Please give us the strength and perseverance to strive to rid our lives of these temptations that hinder our walk with you. your will for us can bring so much joy and peace and when we are in a sin we cannot feel the full presence of you in our lives. Lord, I again give you my weakness with food and ask that you bind Satan away from me and help me with my temptation.

I realize that God uses people even when they are weak and that I will never be perfect with this addiction but my prayer is that God will still use me to speak and witness to women who face this same temptation. The devil is so scared that I am going to get it all together that he keeps throwing things and circumstances in my face. I am so tired of deflecting them. Yesterday I was so good and did only liquid all day long and when I got home to mix my drink at around 4 p.m., I go to the box containing the jars and it is labeled chocolate but guess what all of them are: vanilla. Every time I get my head on straight with this diet I have a fight with my children, my mom has a massive heart attack, my brother shows up at my job asking for help, or the chocolate containers are really vanilla. I was yelling at the devil out loud when this happened, "You are not going to win, leave me alone, I will not cheat, and I will drink the nasty, yucky vanilla tasting junk," out loud at the devil. My poor daughter looked at me like I was having a breakdown. I think from now on I will just shout out loud when the devil is attacking me. It actually felt good to yell at the one who is trying to make me stumble.

I am now writing after being off the liquid diet for over a year. After being off the liquid diet for a year . . . I was so ashamed to admit that I had gained over one hundred pounds back. I let so many people down; my family, my children, myself and most of all, the Lord. Why did I throw away how wonderful I felt for a piece of food? I can't explain how it felt to finally be able to shop in the regular sizes, to go into a thrift shop and buy clothes for two or three dollars because I was little. I really felt amazing, beautiful, and healthy, but I was scared to death of being thin. I never did deal with my head and my thoughts while losing the weight so quickly, and I was not prepared mentally to start eating again. My family and friends joined me in my big meal after almost a year and I literally cried because I did not want to gain it all back. Sadly, and with no one to blame but myself, I was again dealing with a sin that overwhelmed me. I gave all of my "fat" clothes away and really thought that I was going to be okay, but still had not found the key to thinking thin, eating thin, and being able to say no to food.

I have realized that I need to confront a monster from my past that is definitely part of my disorder with food. The Lord has revealed to me over the last eight years in very small pieces that I was abused physically as a child. I believe I experienced inappropriate touching between the ages of four and seven from a family member. I remember being cornered and scared and unable to fight back. I did say, "No," and, "Don't," and, "Leave me alone," to my attacker but no one was there to help me. I know that the Lord has helped me face this to get to the demon that has made me feel unworthy of being pretty, or unworthy of being thin.

The protective coating that fat brought to me started then because, in my mind, the abuse stopped because I became too chubby for the person to abuse me. This probably had little to do with it stopping, but in my young, innocent mind I began to equate being heavy to being safe. I am not four anymore and no one will hurt me sexually, verbally, or physically again. When I was successful and looking good, men didn't do anything inappropriate but would try to encourage me with whistles or telling me how sexy I looked. Even though it was innocently done it really brought up some very serious insecurities that I had not dealt with before because of my size. In Sandi Patty's book, "Layers" she discusses how we protect our inner beings with layers that need to be peeled away before they become prisons. I have been in the prison of being overweight for far too long and I have got to get to the core of the layers and begin to heal.

I am now desperately trying to keep the sixty pounds off that I still lost on the liquid diet. All or nothing seems to be my personality. I had the discipline to not eat a thing for almost a year but can't eat healthy each day. I have got to quit saying, "I can't," "I won't," "I don't know," and start thinking and experiencing the power of God. Just recently I participated in a Bible study about the armor of God (Ephesians 6:11–17) and if we would wake up each day and put on our armor we could conquer anything. If we are saved and have Christ in our lives why wouldn't we want the helmet of salvation to protect our thoughts and mind's? Facing each day holding the shield of faith to deflect what the devil tries to attack us with minute by minute, and the power that brings. God has provided us with all the pieces to protect us in a battle. He knows there is a spiritual war going on in each of our lives, and through His word he gives us all the tools and weapons we need to be spiritual victors.

In the book of Job, the Lord states several times that Job is, "blameless and upright, a man who fears God and shuns evil." (Job 1:8) Even blameless, Satan is allowed to attack Job in all areas of his life to see his loyalty to the Lord. No matter what is thrown at him, Job continues to have faith in God. None of us is blameless in this day and age and yet we question and whine and let the Lord know how tired we are with our struggles. I have come to like being nicknamed Job because I want people to see me as a strong and faithful servant. Job was inflicted with sores and was shunned from his family and friends for his appearance and that is how I have felt since gaining the weight back. Unlike Job I am not blameless, and the self-hate and disappointment I have taken on is very difficult to bear. My family and friends worry about me, and I know the hardship I have caused everyone. I will not be defeated, I will not quit and Satan will not win. I will put on my armor daily and will fight this battle with God on my side. I believe that we need to forgive ourselves in order for this to happen and, "forgetting what is behind and straining toward what is ahead, I press on toward the goal to win the prize for which God has called me." (Philippians 3:13, 14)

> Lord, thank you for your forgiveness, patience, and love. Help all of us who are dealing with an addiction and weakness, Lord. Help us to use the armor that you have provided for us in your word. Guide us, direct us and give us courage to face the devil and his temptations each day. I love you and thank you for answered prayer. Amen.

TRAGEDIES TURN TO TESTIMONY

> My face is red with weeping, deep shadows ring my eyes; yet my hands have been free of violence and my prayer is pure.
>
> Job 16:16–17 NIV

God has told us through all things to find joy, through all things to find peace, and through trials and tribulations to be thankful. I have always wondered how I am supposed to do this, but lately, as my walk gets closer and my faith is stronger, I do see how this is what God wants. If we truly believe in an omnipotent God—one who is all knowing and loving and works things together for good for those who love Him—then why wouldn't we be at peace with our lives and what we encounter? Now, hear me that we are also to mourn and we are also to feel loss but when we let God take those feelings He will turn them around and give you a peace that a non-Christian cannot understand.

My first realization of how quickly death can happen was when I was fourteen years old. The day before my freshman year in high school, I woke up to my mom screaming—I mean a blood curdling scream that seemed to shake the whole house. She had just been told over the phone that her mother, my Nana, had passed away in the night. She had just been at our home the night before for dinner and she was not in ill health except for lapses in memory and some dementia. She was eighty-four years old and, amazingly, lived a life for Christ and raised my mom in the church. It was so devastating to have no warning, no way to say goodbye and all the things that one wants to say. This was the first viewing and funeral I had ever attended and with it being someone so close to me it was really a difficult time. Back then, you had visitation for three nights from like two to nine and then on the fourth day the funeral service. At nineteen, my Papa, my mother's father, had to move into our home to slowly die of cancer. He was ninety-one and the closest thing to a saint that I have ever been around. Now I know we are all saints according to God's purpose, but he was one holy saint. My mother lovingly took care of her father for about six months until he passed away. I truly believe no matter how long you have to say good-bye it still isn't enough time. Not having the opportunity with Nana and then watching Papa suffer were both very difficult in their own ways.

Through my life I have had to watch many people in my family die. One of them was my uncle who died from cancer while we all stood around his bed and sang hymns his last few days on this earth. Another loved one was my brother-in-law who died from cancer at a young age of fifty-six, an awful cancer that eats at your body. But the one that took my breath away was my precious daddy. You have to understand that I was daddy's baby girl, the youngest of four and absolutely adored my father. He was someone I could always lean on and look to for advice and just always loved me no matter what I had done. He was seventy-three when he died and the two years before his death he would call me at 6:30 a.m. every morning to wish me a great day at work and to tell me he loved me. He was my human alarm clock. My son was born in 1994 and we named him after my dad because of how much Jeff and I both loved him. I believe having my son helped dad to live a little bit longer to love on his namesake.

The memories of my father are so wonderful to me and the fact that I had such a strong father figure in my life made it harder for me to let go of my earthly father and lean on my heavenly one. Through his death I went through a huge depression that without that phone call each morning I didn't want to get out of bed. Five months after daddy past away I was put on an antidepressant to get me through the day. This was very difficult for me because being raised in such a strong Christian home the belief was that if you leaned on the Lord and gave him everything then you didn't need drugs to get through. I have since changed from that drug to another one, lexapro, but I strongly believe that there are times in our lives that we have to be smart and use what doctors have to offer. My dad was everything to me and watching him die from emphysema was a devastating blow that God is still helping me through even nine years later. The testimony that I would give from my relationship with my dad would be that we need to always put our relationship with the Lord first and not lean on anyone on earth. Our Creator is the only one that knows all of our needs and can guide us without human feelings that just get in the way.

All of these deaths were pretty well expected but I will never forget the Memorial weekend of 1999. One of my dearest and closest friends, Gail, was going to experience one of the worse ordeals in the world. I had been with this sweet family just the week before to celebrate my friend's sister's birthday, and on the next Friday night I was cropping with another friend, putting memories and pictures together on paper. Anyway, my mother and sister had been sent to find me because Gail's sister had been killed in an automobile accident that evening and Gail had asked for me. Not only was her sister killed but her sister's husband as well and their baby boy, fourteen months old was in an I.C.U. at our local children's hospital. I was in such shock at the news. My immediate concern was to hold my friend and be there to support her and her family.

Those dear Christian parents sat there with their son, John, and their daughter, Gail, who had her husband and two children with her and literally hundreds of people in the waiting room that weekend who had come to pray with them. All of us didn't know what to do but show our support. The baby did not make it, so three days after losing her sister; Gail also had to say good-bye to a chubby adorable nephew. The outpouring of love and support was so wonderful for this family, the one that was my second home from age sixteen to about twenty-one. But how do you survive that, how do you lose an entire section of your family and carry on. I know that these dear people still have awful days missing Amy but I also know instead of turning into bitter hateful people that they are witnessing and still loving the Lord more than ever. It is the daily walk, the daily desire to be Christ-like and also to know that their loved ones were believers and that they are in heaven awaiting our arrival that has seen all of us through. In James 1:12, he states that we all need to stand the test, and these dear Christian friends have done just that and have been fine examples of how to move on through tragedy and glorify God.

I am in the process of reading, A Grace Disguised, which is written by a man, Jerry Sittser, who in one tragic car accident lost his mother, his wife and his four year old little girl. This book so reminds me of that awful weekend for the family I knew, and with his words he reaches out to others who have lost something in their own lives. He reasons that all loss is tragic and without God's grace none of us can, "... use those circumstances to begin a new life. One marked by spiritual depth, joy, compassion, and a deeper appreciation of simple blessings."

In August of 1989 my husband and I realized I was pregnant with our second baby. We had a two year old little girl and were so excited by this surprising news. I say surprising because when we got married I was told that I possibly would have trouble having children because of my size and my cycle. But four years into the marriage we got pregnant with Suzie and didn't have to use any help but just relaxed that our family was in God's hands and we would have children when He wanted us to. I know that sounds cliché, but I truly did not worry about when or why but just left it in God's hands. Anyway, once you have a successful pregnancy you never think you might have a problem with the next one. I thought that most miscarriages happened with the first pregnancy, so when there was a problem with this one it was surprising. I had done a home pregnancy test and found out I was pregnant—I thought I was about two months along actually before I checked.

God's awesome protection for me during this time was so amazing that all I could do was trust in Him. I was starting a new teaching job at a new school and didn't know anyone. I was trying to be on my best behavior when on the second day of work I collapsed in the hallway. Another math teacher who was also new to the school heard my scream and came running to help me. The ironic part of this was that I had trouble the night before with pain and some spotting and didn't realize how devastating the signs were. Before I collapsed I had called my doctor to let him know what was going on and he said he wanted to see me right away, but how do you leave your second day of a new job? I told him I would get there right after work and walked into the hallway to immediately double over. I had been through labor before, and had been through some sicknesses in my life, but the pain I felt at that moment was indescribable. I knew I was losing the baby but I didn't realize how serious my condition was; I found out later that when I doubled over was when the tube actually burst.

Of course my four bosses came running to the lounge where I had gotten to a couch and someone had already called an ambulance. The tough part was sharing with the paramedics that I was pregnant without wanting my principals to find out. Not many people want to hire someone and then find out they are pregnant right away so I was scared to death that I would lose my job. This was not my first ambulance ride, but probably my most critical one. The poor man was trying so hard to get an I.V. in my arm he had straddled the stretcher, and I was doubling in pain and we were going about 95 miles an hour down the highway. He finally got the I.V. in my arm and because of so much trauma he felt responsible for, which he definitely wasn't, he came the next day to the hospital with a plant. I will never forget the kindness he showed me in one of my biggest valleys.

After hours at the hospital, they finally told us that I had a tubal pregnancy and was about ten weeks along when my tube burst. I had over a pint of blood in my abdomen and lost the baby and the tube. I have a nephew the same age as my baby would be, and every time I look at him I think of the baby we lost. Our baby would be nineteen today, and even though I still question why, I know God saved my life and showed me that He was my provider. You see, if I wouldn't have worked that first day at a new job then I wouldn't have had medical insurance for this emergency. Because I did just work that one day, everything was covered. I do not believe it was a coincidence and have no doubt that at any time during that pregnancy I could have lost the baby. I do know without any doubt that God kept me safe until I would be covered with insurance. That still makes me feel so special. I know God provides for me hourly, but that was such a profound statement to how much He loves me and how important I am to Him. My school was lovely and treated me like they had known me forever and I was able to return back to work two and a half months later. It was a great loss but with the Lord and His infinite timing we were taken care of.

About thirteen years ago I taught at a different public school than the one previously mentioned. I was walking to the teacher's lounge and heard a gun go off. Unlike any other time in my teaching career I actually went the other way. I had broken up fights, been cursed at, and had done my share of dealing with violent situations, but I could not deal with a gun. I continued to the lounge and by then everyone in the building knew what had happened. I was in a school where we had gun detectors and security guards but believe me if a student wants to get a weapon in they will. I was at this school for two years and I had just been back from maternity leave so I had a baby at home; I was in survival mode. My family had to hear on the radio that there was a shooting at my school and had no way of knowing if I was safe. We could not call out because all the lines were busy and it was long before cell phones became popular.

I found out later that morning, that a girl had gone up to her ex-boyfriend from behind and blown his head off. Even though the school was about 1,400 children in size, I did know both of these children and it was so difficult to continue out that year with such a tragedy hanging over us all. Those were children I had not been able to help, to encourage, to detour that awful day. It is so hard to watch young people destroying their lives but if we as Christians do not influence the public school system, it is only going to decline even more. In order to be a light in the dark, to be salt of the eath and to witness to sinners we have to be there among them. I urge you to not get so closed off from the sin of this world that you don't do what we are charged to do and that is to feed His sheep. We are to protect our families, raise them up in godliness, but we are also to be the witness to those in darkness.

Being entrenched in two wonderful churches has left me so many dear people to love. So many people that felt like family, special pretend aunts and uncles, unique pretend grandparents have gone on to heaven to be with God for eternity. It is so awesome to know that they are family, that we are brothers and sisters in Christ and that we share a wonderful bond. We know that when we say goodbye to our loved ones, who are

Christians, it is only for a short time before we are reunited in our everlasting home.

The real sorrow is to see young people take someone's life who didn't know the Lord. I have such a burden to reach out to young people to let them know things are not hopeless, that there is someone who cares. There are so many broken homes, so many drugs, alcohol and abuse that I would beg everyone reading this to pray for our children who aren't raised in homes where even the name Jesus is mentioned. Unbelievably there are people in any normal city in America that don't even know what Easter is about.A more recent tragedy for our family was with one of those special uncles to our children. A friend that I had known since I was about eight years old grew so close to not only me but also my husband that he was a groomsman at our wedding. Goober was his nickname and to be honest with you it fit him to a tee. He was lovable, funny, dependable and really one wonderful guy. Everyone loved him and he brought humor and joy to any room he walked into. Goober was a guy who whenever anyone needed a bear hug he would gladly oblige. About two years before my husband passed away he was in a coma from an episode of low blood sugar. We had to put Jeff on a ventilator and pray that he would wake up, it was touch and go for about a week, but he did come out of it with not much damage at all. Goober was there every day after work to make us laugh and to see his buddy. He was so committed to helping his friend get better and recover.

It was just three months later that Goober found out that he had Leukemia—after a year of treatment, a stem cell transplant, and an awesome fighting spirit, the Lord took Goober home to heaven. What is hard to comprehend is how quickly some are taken while others suffer for years. It is healthy to just talk to God about it. Clear the air, so to speak, and He will give you peace.

Tragedy does not always mean death. One such tragedy would be what my dear mother has had to endure over the past eight years. She has had two strokes and two heart attacks since burying her husband of 51 years. She has thankfully survived all of these health issues. It was very tough to see a woman I have seen all my life play the piano like an angel not able to sit up, feed herself or to walk, let alone try to play again. But thankfully God has answered many prayers and she is now walking with a cane and has attempted the piano playing and seems to be better than she has in a long time. Her last heart attack was almost a year ago and the doctors basically told us while she laid in I.C.U. that we would possibly lose her that evening. However, they did not know how hard headed our momma is, she was not ready to go and the good Lord was not ready to take her.

Illness is a very challenging thing to face and as we face it, we again can make a choice of either growing closer to Jesus or becoming a bitter human being with no joy or contentment. Strokes tend to make a person insecure and fearful for what lies ahead and mom has struggled with those doubts and has questioned why she is still here on this earth not able to do much for herself. She continues to fight back and prays constantly for her family and friends and chooses to not give up on what God wants to use her for.

This past Sunday, March 8, 2009, marked another tragedy that made national news, but also hit much closer to home for my church family. I went to church like any other Sunday and had no idea what some had heard already. My pastor shared what had happened that morning. He had been contacted and told that a dear friend of his, who was a pastor of another Baptist church, had been shot in his church at the beginning of the service. This forty-five year old pastor who had served in that same church for twenty-two years was gunned down by a man who he had never met. The man just randomly picked this church. My pastor, with tears in his eyes, asked us to pray for his friend, his friend's family, and his friend's church. Another martyr for the kingdom is with the Lord.

Dear members of that pastor's church went to the family of the man who killed their pastor and had the grace and love to pray with them and ask them if there was anything they could do. I know that is what we are called to do, to forgive and to witness but to do this just hours after the tragedy truly shows how we are to react. My pastor was quoted in the paper that his friend was so Christ-like that he would have forgiven this man immediately for what he had done. This tragedy was so sudden, so meaningless—but God will use all of this for His kingdom. All of the news about this incident was seen nationally by non-believers. People everywhere saw how this church family responded and how, we as Christians, may not understand why tragedies happen but that we have faith in the Lord and we know He will see us through. What a testimony this was to this pastor's life.

The last tragedy I need to mention is the death of my husband. Jeff was diagnosed with diabetes at the age of twenty-seven and being the hardheaded red head that I loved dearly he did not comply. He did not quit smoking, did not take his medicine consistently, and did not watch his diet. He had seen relatives who had diabetes not comply and not be severely affected. Unlike them, his body did not respond well to ignoring this awful disease.

Jeff was athletic and healthy, and what diabetes did to his body in just a short time was unbelievable. For the last three years of his life it was one struggle after another: not being able to walk, being incontinent, vomiting that was non-stop and just overall feeling awful. Through all of this Jeff used his hard-headedness to his benefit—he never gave up and would not quit. In his last months in the hospital he was put on dialysis three times a week for kidney failure, and would not have survived two weeks without it. I wasn't sure what God's timetable was for Jeff but again I knew whatever reason, we were all going through this so God would use it for His glory if we would only let Him.

Jeff was put on a feeding tube the day before I had to go back to work. It was to supplement his nutrition. At first he was put on for twelve hours a day but after four days they found that wasn't enough and he was connected for the full twenty-four. The past few weeks of his life seemed more painful for him with his sores not only on his hips and bottom but now on his legs as well. He seemed to not fight like usual and as I went back to work with less time to see him it seemed a lot more depression had settled in.

> Lord, please help me remember that you are the one in charge. That whatever happens, to let you walk me through. I have always clung to the "Footprints" saying because I can visually picture you carrying me through these difficult times and I just want to thank you for your infinite love that sees me through each tragedy in my life. Your wisdom and counsel in times of suffering are all I need to carry on. Thank you Lord for the joy you can bring out of sorrow. I love you so much. In Jesus' name I pray. Amen.

I worked for about two weeks and during that time Jeff definitely took a turn for the worse. His body had gotten an infection from his sores and no matter what; the doctors could not help him. No dialysis would save him, he wouldn't live through any more surgery and it was now when they told me that he probably had less than a week to live. After such a long illness you begin to wonder if you will ever hear those words and then after you do you can't believe it. I was called from school on a Friday morning because decisions at the hospital had to be made and I needed to be there. It was that afternoon that I had to face my husband and tell him the truth, that his infection had turned septic and that there was nothing more they could do and he would die within the week. The look on Jeff's face I will never forget. He was in shock, he never wanted to face his illnesses and he never wanted to give up. This news really was so hard for him to hear and he quietly cried with me, his mother and his step-mother who were also in the room. Without the Lord giving me the words to say I could not have survived that conversation. God's help and strength is so incredible and He is never late in your need. We stayed with Jeff constantly that week and the last thing he said on Monday was to our twelve year old son, at that time, when Jesse said, "I love you Daddy ," Jeff said, " I love you too buddy." That was it. He slipped into a state where his eyes glazed over and he was slowly leaving his earthly body.

That Monday night was absolutely like walking through hell. They were trying to give Jeff medicine to make him comfortable but he was in such pain he literally grabbed out to me in anguish in a sort of coma state. I cried out to God to please help the nurses find something to help him be at peace until Jesus took him home. Finally about 5 a.m. Tuesday morning Jeff got comfortable and we watched him breathe much easier. He was no longer crying out in pain and he was just lying there while we all waited for God's timing.

Dear friends and family were around his bed his last night, and we were again singing hymns, just like with

Uncle Jack, and prayerfully asking God to take him home. It was about 9:45 a.m. Wednesday when I finally said to him, "Jeffrey, honey, we are so tired of watching you struggle to breathe. Please go on and go see Jesus." About ten minutes later he took his last breath. God is so powerful and awesome and Jeffrey's suffering ended that day. He is whole and perfect in heaven without any pain or sickness.

We all have issues that we are dealing with in this loss. Our children are so different and each is facing this in their individual way but as we go through this sorrow we must not grow apart. We must bond together in Christ's love and lean on each other, and the Lord to see us through. Thanksgiving was one of Jeffrey's favorite holidays because he loved to eat and he loved seeing his extended family. The first holiday is very difficult after losing a loved one but if you are in a fog for that first year the second one seems even more difficult. The first Christmas we put more lights on the outside of our house than ever before, in his memory, because he loved to do that for his home. The more lights the less depression, but that didn't seem to work. I am praying constantly for my children and myself to grow stronger from this heartache and not let Satan have any foothold in this family.

Please remember that everyone in this world is going through something—even people who look like they have it all together don't. As Christians, we need to show people in the world that through anything we have a peace and strength unlike any other. Jeffrey's funeral was a praise service and a witness to anyone there who did not know the Lord. My prayer was that someone would be touched by the words the pastor had to say. Jeff had several friends who are not believers and I wanted them to hear about salvation and what they needed to do to see their friend again.

Jeff was buried on September 11th. I didn't even realize the significance until that morning. All of the preparation and things that needed to be done kept me from realizing what importance that day would have had for Jeff. He loved his country and served as a marine for six years. To be buried on a day that recognizes all of the heroes who were lost during that devastating event on 9/11, and for the ones who have fought for this country since, would have meant so much to him. It helped me see the Lord's hand in this tragedy and that His timing is always perfect.

> Lord, thank you so much for Jeffrey's life, for our twenty-seven years together, for our beautiful healthy children and for just being there through it all. We definitely shared the good, the bad and the ugly. Even through the most difficult times we loved each other and I know that you have blessed me through our relationship and because of it my love and bond with you is so much stronger. Thank you for continuing to help us through this difficult time and for your love and guidance. In Jesus' name. Amen.

DIVORCE IS DENIED

> I have kept to his way without turning aside. I have not departed from the commands of his lips.
>
> Job 23:11, 12 NIV

I strongly believe that in the marriages of this world everyone is under the opinion that spouse's are shirts we will try on. They fit well for awhile but if they shrink, stretch, or get holes we will just throw them away and buy another one. Whatever happened to the marriages that lasted fifty-one years (my mom and dad) and the ones that lasted sixty-two years (my grandparents)? I know it is sin, and I believe that we have forgotten what the vow on the altar truly means.

I am not real sure who said the D word first in our marriage but I do believe that once it is out there that it is really hard to take back. It is like once you say it out loud then you think it is an option. There are so many Christian marriages that have fallen apart for so many different reasons and I haven't got a degree in marriage counseling or a doctorate on behavioral disorders, but I have lived through some major ordeals in my marriage and I was determined to continue no matter what the cost.

God hates divorce. Now, if you have been through a divorce please don't shut the book, I am not judging you, and I don't know your situation. What I am trying to tell you is God can heal anything and any situation. So many times we get caught up in the thought that we deserve better. That God would not want us to suffer with a husband who is mean, angry, jobless or verbally abusive, but I say we do not have the right to say that because Jesus suffered more in His ministry than we will ever suffer on earth. Okay, so if you are in a physically abusive marriage I do not want you to think I am telling you to stay and take it. Absolutely not. Seek help and counseling and be separated while this is going on so you are safe. There are always extreme cases that require specific things, but all I can attest to is what has happened in my marriage and that God has gloriously brought healing to my heart. I honestly can say I loved my husband and am glad we stayed together through it all.

Jeff and I dated for four years, during which short break-ups occurred and one biggie that was about four months long, but, we always seemed to come back together, eventually getting married in 1983. The wedding was of course beautiful, the church was packed and we were blessed with being married by the same pastor who married my parents. We got married three weeks after my college graduation knowing that we would be fine financially. I would get a teaching job in the fall and even though Jeff had only had his job for three months we were going to be great. Yeah, right. Well, as you can guess no job came my way in the fall and immediately we were dealing with financial problems. At twenty-one and twenty-two and, both of us coming to the marriage straight from our parents home, we were about as prepared for what lay ahead of us as a newborn baby. We were in for some growing up and fast.

I believe we had been married just about two years when I first found pornography magazines under our bed. I was the most naive woman in the entire world; I had no idea what they were, and I had never encountered anything like it before. When confronted, my husband said they belonged to a friend and it was no big deal, he would get rid of them and never do it again. I believed him. I had no idea at that time in my life what an awful addiction pornography was and that it was such a big deal. There were tears and confusion in the days ahead but I believed in my husband and we went on. I don't think Jeff understood the pain that the magazines caused, especially when I was overweight and insecure sexually.

I am not sure if the magazines were gone or if Jeff just got better at hiding them but pornography did not come back into our marriage until many years later. I remember at about ten years into our marriage, I found some movies that were not labeled and not out in the open when it began again. I put the movie in the VCR and was horrified at what was on the screen. How could my husband do this? Especially when we had a little girl about six years old, who could have easily put in the movie by mistake? Again, in my stupidity I didn't realize that the addiction was escalating from magazines to movies.

Pornography is adultery. If a man or woman is looking at someone lustfully outside of marriage than the wedding vows have been broken. While I do believe that adultery is the only reason for a divorce biblically, I again believed in my husband and listened to him when he asked me for forgiveness. Of course this was again the "first time" he had ever done such a thing.

I will never forget the third time this entered my home, or should I say the third time God allowed me to witness it. It was the Thanksgiving after my dear daddy had passed away. I woke up to go to the bathroom at about 6:30 a.m. and my husband was so involved in the computer that he did not hear me walking out of the bedroom. There again, to my shock and dismay, were pictures on the screen that turned my stomach. After our fighting ordeal we had to go to my family get together and I had to pretend nothing happened. Of course there were lots of tears, but I let everyone think it was because daddy wasn't there. My husband, because of his diabetes, had been impotent for quite awhile and he claimed he was trying to see if anything worked. By this time in our marriage we had two beautiful children and no matter how often I screamed divorce I could never follow through with it because of my ultimate belief that marriage was for better or worse, sicker or poorer, till death do us part.

Unbelievably I stuck around and there was a fourth

time. My stupidity through this whole obsession was that I did not demand counseling for Jeff, that I thought each time would be the last. Do not be that stupid if you or your spouse have this addiction, seek Christian counseling immediately. Do not wait, ignore, and hide your eyes to how sick and depraved it is to a marriage. The fourth time sadly had to include my fifteen year old daughter and because of that brought a separation to our marriage that was long overdue. We had so much hurt and so much pain and we needed serious time to pray and seek help from our pastor and Christian counseling if we were ever going to heal our marriage and our family.

I had been away on vacation for a week without the kids or Jeff when I was confronted with the fourth incident of pornography. The minute I walked in the door my daughter dragged me into the bedroom to tell me what she had accidentally seen on the computer. She had innocently thought they were music videos but instead they were videos of sickening sexual acts on the computer screen. The videos were saved on the desktop, right where all of us could see. She was so afraid I would blame her and she had no idea where the pornography had come from. I told her I would talk to her later and that I would handle the situation. I stayed in the house for a week praying fervently about what I should do. Well at fifteen, an innocent young lady, she was not going to let me forget about this or live with it. I let her know how I was prayerfully waiting on the Lord and when He gave me an answer then I would follow His will. It was a week later when I told Jeff that we had to separate, that we needed time to work through so many heartaches, and such build-up that we needed a hammer and chisel to get us free to have a godly marriage. We were separated for almost a year when Jeff came back into the house with God's help. We were together again for the last three years of Jeff's life. It was a very difficult time because not much had changed in Jeff's behavior, but I had changed. I had forgiven Jeff and knew that I did not want him to die alone without his family surrounding him.

> Lord, please touch anyone's heart that is dealing with this awful addiction. Lord let them see how much of a stronghold it is. I ask you to release them of this addiction and to bind Satan from their desires and help them to heal. Please Lord convict where necessary and open eyes all over so that marriages can be put back together and the sanctity of the marriage vows be restored. In Jesus' name, Amen.

Another challenge we had was a different view on alcohol and how much was acceptable. Before we got married we had established that we would never have liquor in our home. This was how I was brought up and I believed it was the best way to raise a family. I know that many people believe it is okay to drink but not to get drunk but I say it is best not to be tempted at all or be a stumbling block for others.

I didn't object if Jeff just had one drink over an evening but it was when he would go to friend's parties without me and come home really late and had clearly had more than one drink. He would often go to bars and play fooz ball with the boys and I wouldn't know where he was for hours. This was also during periods of unemployment for Jeff when he didn't need to get up for work and could party as late as he would like. The drinking became a really big problem when he didn't show at all one night. He had our only car with him and he didn't call or come home. I was seven months pregnant with our first child and when I woke up to get ready for work, I realized I had no way to get there. I will never forget how embarrassing it was to call my mom at 7:00 a.m. and ask her to come drive me to work. When asked if there was something wrong with my car, I had to tell her the truth. She quickly came and got me to work, and all day long I knew that I was going to leave Jeff and go home to my folks. I went to my parents for about two days and after a lot of apologizing and talking from Jeff, I went back to our apartment.

Even though this is all very difficult to share I want everyone to know how magnificently God can heal a heart. How gloriously He can help you surrender all to Him to put the pieces back together if we will just let Him. I am begging you to open your heart to what I am trying to share, that no matter what you are facing, that no matter what the challenge, that you will be willing to try again with God's help.

Drugs became a problem much later in our marriage. As a teenager Jeff had done drugs—very hard ones—and he had openly shared this with me while we were dating. I knew he was a changed man. I, again, was the little naive wife who had maybe seen a joint once and didn't even recognize a bong when I saw one at a party. Jeff maybe didn't practice these things anymore but he was willing to still be in places where it was going on, and still associate with friends who were not Christians leading a totally different lifestyle. I do strongly believe that we are to befriend unsaved people, that we need to have relationships with them, but we do not have to be in a situation where there is so much ungodliness going on that you as a Christian feel uncomfortable. Jeff insisted I go to a party once—I felt like I was at Sodom and Gomorrah and that at any moment the police were going to break in and arrest us. We, as Christians, need to draw the line somewhere between association and condoning what others do. Remember we are not of this world.

I am not sure if Jeff did anything along the way with drugs in our marriage, but with what happened in the last two years of his life I would be surprised if it hadn't happened earlier. After Jeff had come back home after the separation, he was very sick. Basically, he had not been able to work for the last seven years of his illness and had been in and out of the hospital during that time. He was admitted more than forty times before his last stay which was for almost nine months before he passed away. So when I say he had been very sick it really doesn't describe the situation. We had episodes of so many things but during a time of extreme pain and nausea, when Jeff would sit outside for hours and smoke cigarettes on the front step of our house, he decided to smoke a little bit of something else. I know some of his friends gave Jeff drugs to try to help him but this was not going to be done in our house.

This was an awful time. I just didn't understand how Jeff, after we were trying to work things out, would do such a thing. He would make pipes out of aluminum foil and hide them in places in the house. He even went so far as to try to melt his pain pills to put in a needle and shoot it into his arm. The final straw was when Jeff got high and fell in the kitchen and hit his head on the table. After hours in an emergency room and ten stitches he did finally admit to me what he had done. I had put up with it for months but after that I told him with a seventeen and ten year old in the house that if it happened again we would separate. After that night Jeff was never caught again and I believe the fall did scare him but, I continued to find drug paraphernalia for months.

God is so good, God is so helpful and God is so constant. He always let me know, He always tried to give me a heads up with things in my life, but because I didn't handle them with God's help, they continued to happen over and over again.

Jeff came from a divorced family and was raised with four parents because they both got remarried pretty quickly. He always would say divorce wasn't an option, he always would pretend things were okay or no big deal. I do believe divorce is not an option but to continually have situations where God is clearly not at the center of the problem doesn't help build a solid godly marriage. We went to counseling several different times, mostly pastors who would counsel us for free.

Each time we seemed to be okay for awhile but then something else would happen. The things I am bringing up about Jeff are just the biggest things, I again have a temper, I am hard headed, I am a bad housekeeper and I am not a good cook so I am not innocent but the really big things that we have encountered were brought into the marriage by Jeffrey. See, when I am really serious I call him Jeffrey.

Looking back on our years, I can see that we made so many mistakes from the beginning. Both of us were Christians but neither of us was really walking with the Lord. We went to church, we did things with the youth group, and we looked like we were doing everything right. We did some really stupid things when we were dating. I have been in youth work forever and now truly believe that going out in groups is the only way to date as a young person. Tempting each other to do things that are ungodly does not help a relationship but breaks it down. One of the more innocent embarrassing moments when we were dating happened in the parking lot of a monastery, which was not realized until later. I was in the driver's seat and Jeff was in the passenger seat and there was a console in between us. We also had another young couple in the back seat while we were sitting there parked. Jeff and I really were just talking but the windows fogged up from simply our breath and we did not realize someone was approaching the car. I jumped about two feet in the air when someone knocked on my window. When I lowered the window there stood a monk asking us to please not use their parking lot for such things. I think I turned ten shades of red as I apologized and we pulled away. Don't put yourself in that position and don't let your children have too much freedom because they don't know how to handle it.

We didn't read the Bible together or have prayer time together. We weren't putting God first and how can a marriage do anything but struggle when you don't have the one who invented the whole concept in the center? It seemed like all throughout the marriage we would never grow spiritually at the same time or that when one was growing the other was growing in a total opposite direction. Satan really does not want a strong Christian home to develop and he will put any obstacle in your path to keep you from having that kind of home. The problem with us was we never, except at counseling, would pray together over issues—we always prayed separately. "What God has joined together" is what we say on the altar that beautiful wedding day, but I don't believe enough couples understand that the most important thing to join together is your walk with the Lord.

I have mentioned in this chapter the huge issues that Jeff and I dealt with over the years. I am not going to go into who didn't put the lid back on the toothpaste or who left their clothes lying around because I don't believe those little things should be an issue. Please do not blow things out of proportion but do recognize serious issues that need to be confronted. Don't hide behind the idea that if you don't face it it will go away. Because it won't. Sure we had day to day problems, loud obnoxious fights. I can cut someone down with my tongue, but over the last three years of Jeff's life, God helped me control my tongue more.

Jeff was in the marines and because of those six years I believe his vulgar language became a little bit freer. What was hard was when he would curse at me in the car on the way to church in front of the children, and then fifteen minutes later in the church pew amen what the preacher had said. When my daughter was older she let me know that those times really confused her, and she didn't understand why he could do that. I just told her that everyone's heart is not pure but when they walk in church God can touch even the hardest heart and cause anyone to praise him.

It doesn't matter how long you have been married and how much trouble you have been through because God can change any heart that is willing to change. That is the key: both of you need to change. Each heart has to be open to what God wants you to hear and each one of you will need to grow individually and as a couple with the Lord. Christian counseling is the only answer in my opinion because any secular counselor might give you the green light to get a divorce and not to try again. When your marriage has been through so much garbage, and baggage and turmoil you must be patient to let it heal, and mend and grow to be the meaningful marriage that God would want it to be. All of us need to show the same mercy and grace to our spouse that God continually shows us.

We hurt our Savior all the time, we neglect Him, we don't take care of His house, we don't spend quality time with Him and all God does is continue to love us and to cherish us and is consistently there for us when we turn to Him. How can we say we are striving to be holy and treat our spouses like we hate them? You may experience a time in your marriage where you are not in love with your spouse, but continue to love them with Christ's love and you will be able to stay together to move towards a better marriage. Love is a choice in a marriage because that gooey love doesn't last. We have to choose each day to show the love we have been shown since we accepted the love of Christ in our hearts.

> Lord, please touch all the hearts out there that are hurting. Let them feel your presence and guidance. Help them to give you their marriage and truly give you all their hurt and pain. Please let them have hope and faith that all things can be restored with your help. Thank you, Lord, for healing my heart. In Jesus' name, Amen.

Before our separation there was also something else going on besides the pornography problem; Jeff had started to gamble. I couldn't believe after everything we had gone through with my brother who is an addicted gambler that Jeff would start this sin. Early on in our marriage we had gone a few times to the horse races with twenty dollars and enjoyed watching the horses run, or we would play penny poker with friends and had fun with these innocent things. Then, when we found out about my brother eleven years ago with his gambling problem and that his life had been a lie for about thirteen years Jeff and I quit doing anything that involved gambling. It has nearly destroyed his life but his wife continues to stand by him and with God's help will heal their marriage. John was clean for about five and a half years until a few months before Jeff died. My brother was leading a Celebrate Recovery group through his church, had spoken on radio stations and was also a guest on The 700 Club. My brother's life was turning around as he allowed God to lead. But with all addictions the devil never stops trying to rob and destroy each individual's life. Satan has gotten a foothold with John again and he is struggling daily.

A few months before Jeff died my brother made a huge mistake and started gambling again. John's sin of gambling has been very difficult to watch all these years. Everyone kept this from me until after I buried Jeff and then that afternoon I was told about my brother. He loved Jeffrey and was sobbing at the funeral and it was not only over the loss of his brother-in-law but it was also over his sin and failure to walk with the Lord. The Lord was using his life so abundantly and the devil got a foothold and is literally destroying my brother's life again. Two days after I buried my husband I got a phone call early in the morning that my brother had attempted suicide. He has been in such a bad place and has clearly been in need of so much love and forgiveness from the Lord and his family, yet he has never been ready to receive it. All of us need to remember that once we have repented and given the Lord our sin that it is gone. God shows us grace and mercy every time but if we do not forgive ourselves the devil uses that to not let us truly let it go. Please receive and accept forgiveness for yourself in your own mind and when you are tempted remember that you are a child of the King and that you can stand mightily against that temptation.

We must help one another and be there not only physically but spiritually. I know the only one who can help John is Jesus and he has not surrendered it all to him again. He is battling so much guilt, denial, sin and a self-destruction that until he is ready to face himself he will not recover again. I will continue to pray for my brother and I know God is in charge and can do all things if we only allow it. We need to quit struggling and relax and accept that God is all we ever need. No amount of money, no wonderful job, and no prestigious friends are what we need to live abundantly. All we need is our wonderful counselor and everlasting Father, Jesus Christ to see us through.

So back to my story about Jeff. I found something in the mail—the account balance of an account that I knew nothing about, God again revealed a lie and a problem in our marriage. Jeff had opened up a secret account and was using that money to gamble. He went to the boats during the day while I was at work. The anger and hurt I felt at that moment was devastating. I not only had been through so much with my brother but I also couldn't afford food for the family let alone money Jeff was just throwing away.

After praying over what I had found out I called our pastor to ask him for advice. We decided that the next time we met for counseling, that in front of our pastor I would bring up the secretive account. Jeff, because of his illness or medication, was getting more erratic and violent so I wanted to have someone else in the room to help with the confrontation. It was just like all the other things, it was no big deal and he wouldn't do it again and I was blowing it out of proportion. When you keep getting told the same thing over and over for twenty years you start to wonder if you are the one causing the problems, if you do blow things out of proportion. All of these problems with Jeff always brought the Lord and me closer together. The account was closed and I am sure he gambled again but after the separation he became too ill to drive.

> Dear Lord, if anyone out there who is reading this believes that gambling is harmless please let them know that it, again, is a strong addiction. That it is destroying families and people's lives. Please help those who have strongholds in their life to let them go and to lean on you. Break the chains that bind us Lord to things that are ungodly and help us to only reach out to you. Thank you, Lord for answered prayers. Amen.

Our sex life throughout our marriage was never a very healthy one, and I always assumed that it was my weight and also my conservative view on what sex should be like. I realize now that the abuse I suffered as a child caused me to not be open minded sexually and that the scars I still carry hurt our marriage. Not remembering what I had gone through made it difficult to get help and by the time I realized what happened to me and the problems it caused, Jeff was impotent. As I look back on our relationship I believe it also wasn't healthy because of the pornography that Jeff was involved in throughout our marriage. After our son was born it was only a few months later that Jeff became impotent due to the diabetes. The last eleven years of our marriage we had no type of physical relationship. It seemed that whenever we would try to do anything and he was unable to he would become so upset that it was just not worth the effort. I would feel so unattractive and vulnerable that I pulled away, and because Jeff couldn't perform he didn't even try, so therefore our physical relationship became null and void.

Intimacy doesn't mean sex, but when there is none of either your marriage quickly gets even worse than before. I would have been perfectly happy with any type of affection but that was not possible from Jeff's point of view. Anytime he couldn't do what he needed to do, then I wasn't going to be satisfied either. Again, this is a very serious problem that many marriages have and counseling needs to be sought after and medical solutions to the problem need to be looked into. We did neither. I have remained faithful to my husband over the twenty-three years of marriage. The only man I have ever been with is Jeff. Even though we did much more than we should have when we were dating I can sincerely tell my children that their father is the only man I have been with and in this day and age I think that is a great testimony. I can't say that I believe Jeff had been faithful. I believe there were two times in our marriage that God tried to reveal to me that Jeff was having other relationships. I can't believe that I would rather stay in the dark than find out things but that is exactly what I did.

The first time was about three years into our marriage and Jeff was staying out later and later from work. He finally did admit to me that he was going to a bar with some people from work and that one of the women confided in him about her problems with her boyfriend. Eventually, he also admitted to kissing this woman but nothing else. I let it go because Jeff quit that job to get away from her and I believed him. Jeff and I stayed together and soon after I became pregnant with Suzie.

The second time was with a girlfriend of one of Jeff's best friends. He totally denied this one but I knew things were not innocent when she started calling the house and asking for Jeff and sending him cards in the mail. What unbelievable boldness. I again was dealing with only a gut feeling and did not catch him in any compromising position. I caught him at her house once and found them in the kitchen just talking. I still feel that something more happened with this woman but I did not pursue this gut feeling and again I just went on and did not face what was happening. I did not want to have to deal with it and the lies. I was not going to divorce Jeff so why try to deal with uncomfortable issues?

In order to heal from something you can't hide it away and not face the scars or the damage that the hurt has caused. That was the biggest mistake I kept making over and over, I just pushed my hurt aside and kept trying to stay together. The staying together part became more important than actually having a godly marriage and one that glorified the Lord. Staying together isn't the point if everyone in the house is miserable. Face your problems and begin to heal.

A constant over the twenty-three years of our marriage was financial difficulties. We started our marriage off on the wrong foot. Remember I didn't get a teaching job and Jeff had just started a job. I did do some substituting and I received a job in the spring of 1984 and have taught since that time. However, Jeff did not hold his job for very long and continued to only work for a few months wherever he became employed. This caused consistent difficulty in paying bills. His temper would be why he would lose a job or just his constant belief that he was too good for certain jobs. He always knew more than his boss and he constantly would share what he thought right before he would quit. While Jeff held any of these jobs, he was a hard worker. However, he would not think before he spoke and would hastily leave a job for any reason.

Eight years into our marriage Jeff got his first job that had great benefits and held a lot of promise. At that time I also shared with Jeff that he had to stay in this job forever, that he could not keep quitting. I was tired of working three jobs and teaching summer school. I guess Jeff believed me when I said I was not going to deal with unemployment anymore and he stayed at that job eight years; it was wonderful and we almost could pay our bills every month on time. After eight years he did quit and worked at a few places before his health became so bad that he couldn't work at all.

I know more and more couples struggle with money issues more than any other problem. In our marriage it caused more fights and anger. I also know that because Jeff wasn't the head of the house financially that it also affected his self esteem and destroyed his confidence in several areas.

I was teaching all day, tutoring for two hours after school, going to be a cashier at a local grocery store until one in the morning, and getting up and doing it all over again. I was tired, angry, and mean because I hated my life. I couldn't believe after working so much that we still struggled. I was leaving my toddler to work three jobs while Jeff lay around all day at home. He didn't even help around the house, do laundry or clean, because of his depression. The pressure of never having enough money to pay your bills is so stressful and it never seemed to end. We both believed in tithing and we both knew that what we had was because God had blessed us, but we went through times of not believing we could tithe when we didn't have grocery money. All I can say is God is so faithful and the times when we tithed we were so protected from bills, and the times we failed to have faith and didn't tithe we struggled more than ever. God can do so much more with 90% than we can do with 100%.

I have not always been wise with money and I have made many mistakes by doing things for our children we couldn't afford, and my way to show love to people is through gifts or sending cards. When God lays someone on my heart I immediately try to do something for them. I know that I contributed to our money problems but the constant unemployment Jeff had was the major reason we had trouble. God directs our paths if we let Him and He will continue to protect me through it all if I continue to be faithful to tithe what is already His.

Through it all Jeff and I stayed together. Amazingly, through God's grace He saw us through. Our relationship for the last six months of Jeff's life was the best it could be. I would go see Jeff almost every day for about three to four hours and try to visit with him while I was there. When school started again my visits were every other day because of homework I had from work and house work I needed to do. Jeff watched television or slept so the conversation was not very lively for most of my visits. Jeff never admitted what was going on with his body. He would not talk about dying and he would not help me with any closure. This used to make me crazy because I didn't want him to have false hope and I would have liked to talk about memories and what was happening but Jeff was in constant denial and would not face any of the facts. I am sure this is why he hung on for so long because he did not give up and continued to fight to his best ability. I decided to stop trying to figure out what was going on and just leave it in much more capable hands than my own, and let the Lord lead our lives.

Who can know what is best besides the Lord? I need to not question why Jeff had been in the hospital almost nine months, six of those to be bedridden, and why he continued to struggle with his pain and depression. I need to be honest with the Lord about my confusion but then I also need to let the Lord know that I understand He is the author of life and Jeff wasn't going anywhere until God allowed it to happen. Our marriage was healed, we prayed together and read the Bible together by his bedside, and we loved each other.

I still am in constant prayer for our children and their anger and resentment of things that have happened through the years. I have to hold on to the fact that I try to do all things through Christ and that he will be faithful in my children's lives. Hopefully, they will not rebel but will be compelled to lean on our Lord Jesus. I consistently tell my daughter not to see a woman who was abused but to see a mother who always strived to be Christ-like. To forgive others like Jesus has forgiven me.

It is so sad that we waited so long to do these things, that we had to have so many things happen for us to totally lean on Him. Please don't wait as long as we did, change your hearts right now. Start anew your relationship with your spouse and the Lord at the same time and both will become bonds you cannot live without.

> Thank you, Lord, for your grace and mercy and your forgiveness for where we have failed you in our marriage. Thank you for keeping us together through the good and the bad times. Lord, please help whoever is reading this and let them know that all things are possible through you and that they should not give up on their marriage. Help all of us to forgive like you forgive and to help each other build up instead of tear down. Thank you Lord for all you have done to restore my marriage. In Jesus' name, Amen.

MINISTRY MOMENTS

> I know that my Redeemer lives, and that in the end he will stand upon the earth.
>
> Job 19:25 NIV

God can use any one of us as long as we continue to walk with Him no matter what the struggle. Even the most unworthy person can be used by God if only we are willing. I have been so blessed to be able to go on so many camps and mission trips that have just changed my life each time. There was one specific mission trip that stands out for strengthening my personal relationship with the Lord. During the trip, I was really convicted to have a walk with the Lord that didn't go up and down but one that was steady and consistent. I reluctantly went on this trip with my new church family about four months after my Dad passed away and came home a much more consistent Christian.

I came home from that trip knowing that even in the really rocky times that I wouldn't plummet in my walk, but I would be secure to know that I was in the

Lord's wonderful arms. It was a trip eight years ago and as a counselor for the young people of my church I was touched right along with all of them at how awesome God is. To get away from the television, the phone, and just the rigors of one's everyday life gave me the time to just give everything to Him, minute by minute. The Holy Spirit's presence was amazing. We would pray for a need and the Lord would always provide. His unfailing love was so evident that I had to repent of knowing Him since I was ten, but not really being His, until the age of thirty-seven. Since that mission trip I still sin and I still make miserable mistakes but I guarantee you that something changed and the peace I have now is beyond comprehension.

When I graduated from college I had a degree to teach Elementary School and a minor in mathematics. When I didn't get a job that fall I had to substitute to try and earn a living. Remember we were newly married and totally unprepared for the real world. Anyway, God used this time to let me see where he really wanted me in my career. I was never called to sub in the elementary grades but was always called to sub high school math. I absolutely loved it. God, in His gentle guidance helped me to see where I could be used for Him and where I would be so happy. I had to go back to school for just three classes and got another degree to teach high school mathematics. No matter how old a child is they just need love and respect. God has given me so many opportunities to witness in a non-threatening way and has even let me see where lives have been changed through my witness to them. What an amazing thing to see someone you have witnessed to with no response and then years later see them praising and worshiping the Lord with the heart of a true believer. I don't, in any way, use my teaching time to preach but I will let them know the very first day of school that no one in my room will say Jesus Christ in that disrespectful way. As the days progress, and someone slips and uses my Lord's name in vain during class my response is, "Yes, please go ahead and pray." Eventually they understand that it is just not done in my presence. I have led the Fellowship of Christian Athletes in my school and have had prayer time in my room weekly during lunch, and we have had many students around the flagpole to pray at the beginning of the school year. Remember this is a public school and, again, all things are possible to those who love the Lord. I hope that no matter what happens to my teaching career that the Lord will use my relationship with young people to grow His kingdom.

As a young person growing up I went on choir trips and youth camps and enjoyed those weeks with my friends and meeting new ones. When I became old enough to be a counselor I then took on that role. I never missed a summer to go and be spiritually fed by the wonderful godly leaders at those camps. I am not one of those adults that can go and feel that everything is for the kids. I am one that is crying and rededicating my life right along with them. I thank God for all the times He has laid things on my heart during those ministry moments with the young people.

I changed churches at the age of thirty-seven and I was going to just sit back and be in the congregation, you know, not share my gift with this new body of Christians, well God had other plans. I couldn't stand being on the sidelines; I wanted to get right in there and do what I was called to do. To work with young people in any way possible. The last nine years have been so pertinent to my walk with the Lord and have helped me not only endure the past few years with a steady firm walk but to rejoice for the walk the Lord has given me.

When Jeff was in a coma one spring I took a sabbatical from teaching my girl's Sunday school class. I felt like I needed to spend the least amount of time possible away from Jeff, so I would just go for the worship service. I had no idea it would turn out to be such a long time—about sixteen months—since I had been working with the youth. I missed it terribly. For two of the last five summers I was unable to go on the camps and mission trips because of Jeff's health and have missed those moments of getting away and just being immersed in God's wonderful Spirit.

We are all called to be ministers the moment we give our heart to the Lord. There is no special place that only can be used for witnessing. God wants all people to see how different we are, how we are set apart. Do the people you work with or go to school with know that you love Jesus? Do they tell dirty jokes around you or curse around you or share inappropriate things with you? Wouldn't it be better to tell them that you are a child of the King and you are not comfortable with those things? We need to be proud of being Christian. Why are we so scared of how people will react? How can God bless us if we don't even act like we know Him? I have my Bible at school on my desk, I have Christian books on my bookshelf and if students ask to look at them I sure do let them. During lunch or after school if they bring up questions about my beliefs I share with them with kindness and truth. People who don't believe do not need an angry confrontation about the sin they are in; they need someone to share that what they are missing is God's peace and forgiveness. Do not spoil opportunities with a prideful heart; humble your heart and let God use you.

The last ten years of my teaching career have been my boldest. As I have already said, I work in a public high school and we all know that the name Jesus is suicidal in the public arena; but, oh how God has blessed my ministry. From the beginning of my career I would tell students, if asked, what I believe and I have constantly prayed that there will be opportunities to witness. It was in 1999 when I purchased two Bibles to give to two senior girls who were graduating. I knew that neither girl was in a Christian home; I was so afraid I would be the last one who would have the chance to give them God's word. God has blessed me by now having one of those girls worshiping with me at my church every Sunday and she is now walking so closely with the Lord. She has married a Christian young man who I also had as a student and has led her younger sister to the Lord. We are still praying for her parents.

Another blessing, God has chosen to send me is a young man who I taught about ten years ago. Scott is such a joy and it has truly blessed my heart to watch him grow in the Lord. I was invited to Scott's older brother's wedding because I had also taught him and was torn with whether I should go or not. It was out of town and I would have to go up just for the wedding and come right back home. My daughter talked me into going and offered to go with me and help drive because eight hours one way was too much for me to handle. Suzie knew how awesome it would be for me to walk into that wedding 160 pounds lighter than I was when I taught this group of young people. Some of them didn't even recognize me and it was really exciting to see past students all grown up.

At the reception, there was liquor and the wedding party and several of my ex-students were getting drunk. It had always been my rule if I was invited to a party of ex-students that I would leave before they got so inebriated that it upset me. Before I left the reception, I had the opportunity to witness to all of the students that were there and one of them was Scott. He was used to me preaching to him and we had several conversations when he was in high school about the Lord. Scott promised me that night that he would come to church with me at least once and see how it was. Scott was raised in a great home with values and two wonderful parents who took him to church as a boy, but he had wandered away from the Lord during his college years.

A few weeks after the wedding, I called Scott and picked him up for church. The Lord spoke to Scott that day and his life totally changed. God has blessed me with a renewed relationship with this young man and he has blessed Scott with a renewed relationship with Him, a new job and a fine Christian young lady that he met at our church, who will become his wife in a few months. Scott says that his brother's wedding, seeing me again and my insistence in him coming to church has changed his life. I did absolutely nothing but share what God laid on my heart at that wedding reception and sit back and watch Him work. Scott is working with the young people at our church and he's truly an example of what God can do if we will simply reach out and invite people to come worship with us.

In 2006 I handed out six Bibles. Hopefully if they have not read them, they will reach out to God's word in the near future. I have students who ask to go to church with me and my walk with the Lord is an open book. I do not preach or condemn but I try to have conversations that are non-threatening with the kids. I want them to know the truth. Most of my students have parents who are letting their children just figure it out on their own. I am so glad that Jesus was always around my home as I was growing up and that I wasn't left on my own to figure out truth and where I was going to spend eternity. I am not sure how many children I have witnessed to through the years, but I do know that even if they didn't make a decision in front of me, I planted a seed that God can use one day to grow.

God has shown me to be open with all students. Don't ever think that someone is just too far gone, because it has been those that God has let me see changed. None of us knows anyone's heart. None of us can tell the pain anyone is in. We need to witness to everyone whenever the door is open and not put up barriers for the ones we think are unreachable. Please quit being a lukewarm Christian and decide right now to not wait 26 years like I did to be on fire with the Lord. I don't want Him to spew me out anymore. I want you to know how wonderful it feels to be walking so close to my Savior that I feel His presence constantly. Thank you God for staying with me through all of my growth and thanks so much for our strong relationship. God does know every heart and God does know every heart-ache, so be open to His leading and speak to anyone who will listen and sit back and watch our Mighty Father at work.

> Lord, please help me to stay on a constant walk with you. Help those who are reading this to realize how amazing you are when we walk with you daily. It is so wonderful to have a consistent conversation with you and the fact that you know me so well. God help me to do your will in my ministry. In Jesus' name, I pray. Amen.

CONFUSED BUT CONNECTED

> Nevertheless, the righteous will hold to their ways, and those with clean hands will grow stronger.
>
> Job 17:9 NIV

It seems no matter how far away I would try to run the Lord would gently bring me back to His loving arms. Many times I wanted to be cut free from our relationship but God would never let me relax or feel okay unless I was with Him, surrounded by His love and care.

Confusion comes in many different forms, it is a word I use when I have no idea what is going on or why, but it is when I am thankful God is in control. Knowing that no matter what I do, or what I mess up, that if I continue to have faith, God will guide me safely home. The fact that our connection will never be cut off gets me through all of the difficult times. The times when I have felt far from God were not when He left me but rather when I had turned away from Him. I believe though that no matter what you do as a sinner, if you have accepted Jesus as your Lord and Savior there is no way to sever that connection. You are forever in His hand and He is always going to be there. God is not, however, a hot-line number that you use whenever you are in trouble; He is a relationship you should have through the good and the bad times. He should be your most important relationship and one that is nurtured and treasured for what He is. You should ask yourself these questions and decide what you could do to make your relationship with the Lord so much closer: How is your connection? Can you hear clearly His voice in your daily decisions? Do you believe that you are important enough to Him that at any moment you can ask Him anything?

One of my sweet students has gotten close with me. She has even gone to church with me and listened to my testimony about Jesus. She told me that one of our senior boys got killed today in a car accident. I was not only confused but numb. This beautiful young African American man had the most wonderful smile in the entire world and he came in my room almost hourly to share it with me. As she was telling me she was crying and all I could say was how sorry I was.

We had deep conversations several times and his life was full of heartache but all he did was smile with two huge dimples and show me so much respect and love. I have to be strong for my students, who will see my response to this tragedy. Aaron and I talked about the

Lord but I don't know for certain if he was a believer, I sure hope that he was and that he is in heaven with our Lord. This type of news is why I can't rest knowing there are so many children out there who don't know Jesus. I have to spend every moment trying to show Christ's love to these young people because we never know what each moment will bring.

> God, please help me use this tragedy to witness to my students. Please be with Aaron's family and help them to lean on you Lord through this time. I am going to miss him Lord and he will truly be missed at school. Please give me every opportunity to share you to the lost people I work with, not just the students but the adults as well. Lord please give me the strength to deal with this unbelievable news and to give my confusion to you. In Jesus' name I pray, Amen.

I just found out that Aaron's wake is going to be held on my 45th birthday. I can't believe that I am going to have to see so much sorrow on a day I am supposed to celebrate. I have had a few days to let his death sink in a bit but I still cannot comprehend why such things happen. God is in control and I know that this tragedy can reach so many young people to the Lord. I pray that God can use me to that end. I teach with a very strong Christian woman. She helps me, listens to me, prays with me and she is the reason my nickname is Job. As I think about the week, month, year or years I have had, I understand why she jokingly calls me Jobetta. I used to think that it was an awful thing to be compared to

Job but then I realized that Job was a truly godly man, that he loved the Lord with all of his heart and that through it all he continued to give God glory. Once I looked at it that way I was actually complimented by the comparison. I just pray that I don't ever turn my back on the Lord and that I continue through all things to stay right there by His side.

I heard a sermon once about suffering for Christ and to feel joy in those sufferings. I can truly say that I don't respond to my troubles by being depressed but I do respond by leaning harder on the Lord. I can't imagine going through day in and day out some of the things that I have encountered without the hope I have. I can't imagine people thinking this is all there is and that there is nothing after death. I know that there is so much to be thankful for and can't wait to be praising God continuously for eternity.

I woke up Monday morning this week to find that a small diamond had fallen out of my wedding ring that I have had for twenty-five years. I continued throughout the day doing a little bit of housework, going to the hospital to see Jeff, taking my son to shop for school clothes, being turned down for a credit card at American Eagle, being told I was the first one that the salesman had to tell was turned down, having a two hour fight with my twelve year old son on what kind of friends he will be allowed to hang out with and ordering Chinese food for dinner, before the Chinese food arrives being called by my niece to come help my sister who is crying hysterically in the background, driving to her house without dinner to find out that her nineteen year old son had treated her terribly and walked out of his house packing to never see her again, coming home three hours later with a terrible headache and laying down to try to go to sleep for some needed rest. That is a fairly calm day in my life. I know we all have days that we can't believe, days that we never think will end but we need to be ready even on those days to help anyone in need and to pray with your sister or a friend who is struggling with an issue in their life. Don' t turn inward, don't be a self-pity partier but show God's love outwardly, reach out to others and you tend to not wallow in your own struggles.

Have you ever felt God telling you to do something? I mean truly knew He was leading you in a certain direction. I had one of these incidents happen about seven years ago. I got involved in a situation at work where I knew God had told me to do something but once I did it everything came crashing in on me. I really, to this day, believe that I did what I was supposed to do but I am confused why it all backfired on me. I was persecuted for trying to do what was right. From that one situation so many bad things have happened to me and my career, but I still feel that I did what God wanted me to do. Sometimes when we stand for justice we will be torn down in the world's eyes. Looking back on the situation I could have handled it differently and maybe not gotten into as much trouble. This incident stayed on my record at my school and along with an incident that happened last year has now found me unemployed. Definitely, confused right now.

I had taught at this high school for fourteen years,

and during that time won awards and was truly loved and respected by my students and the families of the community. That is not enough if you make the man in charge angry at you. Despite your reputation, your commitment and your love for the school and even the fact that you have tenure, any administrator may release you if the correct paper work has been done even if they are all lies on the paper. Last year I reported that my principal had inappropriately spoken to me, that he screamed and demeaned me verbally and I was determined that the Board of Education would know of this incident. My superintendent warned me that I did not want to go in front of the board that I did not want to be a "whistle-blower" but I was determined to do what I thought needed to be done. I was put on a year's probation and told to abide by all of these things.

I started off the year with a new attitude, new principal, and was ready to be "perfect". I didn't realize how badly I was up a creek and how many paddles I did not have. I sponsored the cheerleaders in the fall, worked to the best of my ability and had no idea that people were spying on me and writing down anything they could to pass on to the superintendent. A week before Christmas I was summoned to a meeting with my superintendent to hear him say that he had witnessed enough to recommend that I be terminated. I am really naive and honestly did not see this coming. I really believed that I was indispensable and that the community would not allow this to happen. Through many tears, prayers, and wise counsel from my lawyer, I decided not to fight it, to not have a hearing with the board, to not have my day in court because they would continue to try and get rid of me.

I truly believe that the devil could not stand the influence I had in that building. It was harder and harder to be in a public school with my strong beliefs and see what was being allowed to go on. I was given a list of twenty-three things that were supposedly cause for my dismissal. The list was ludicrous, unfounded, and totally taken out of context. It broke my heart to not be working there. I believe God is still calling me to write and speak and now He has given me the time to do just that. I love the Lord with all my heart and no matter what the devil throws at me I will not turn away and like Job I will continue on even if I feel blameless in the persecution.

Anytime confusion or questioning comes into my heart I ask God to help me let it go, to not worry, to not fear and to let God handle it. It really is a great way to get off the hook, to put it in someone else's hands, someone much more capable to not screw it up. Please give it all to Him, let it go, quit trying to drive and just become a passenger.

One of the most awful times in my life was when I had to leave my church home and find another fellowship. I was so confused how my Lord could allow this to happen and could not fathom what good could come from such a situation. My whole life had been at my church. I was there in the nursery from four weeks on and never missed unless I was sick. Because of my mom being the pianist and my dad being a deacon everyone knew me, it was one great big family and I loved being there. All my memories, during my life were made at that church. I was married there, my parents were married there and all I wanted to do was stay there and be content. God had another plan in mind.

The church was very vibrant all through my life and especially from 1992 to 1996 we had a pastor and music director that were wonderful men of God and the church grew in numbers. My husband and I sang in the choir and Jeff even became a deacon at that time. He was growing spiritually for the first time in our marriage and it was wonderful to see God working in his life. Then, tragedy struck our church; these two men within a year of each other left, and the devil had a field day with the devastation it brought. It was about a year and a half later when we had a new pastor who was a godly man but who was not being supported by the elite of the church. Our new pastor wanted to make some changes but he was continuously stopped by these people who thought they were in control, and not the Lord.

It was through this awful time, when my church family had become controlling individuals who thought church was a country club, that Jeff and I decided to leave. They didn't want to change and because of this my husband and I felt God calling us to stand up for our pastor and do biblically what I had always been taught that you support the man of God in charge of your spiritual body unless he is in a sin against the church or his family. This situation was not the case. I stood up at the last business meeting before they fired our pastor and pleaded with them to not do this. I quoted scripture and warned them that the church would lose several members if they followed through with this. They did not listen and dismissed our pastor. His last Sunday was our last Sunday. It was a decision that was so God inspired, but was honestly in the top five of the toughest things I have ever had to do.

My husband was a deacon for about a year and saw the worst witness at those meetings during this tragic time than he had seen in many years. The fighting and cursing and disruption these older deacons caused was unforgivable. Jeff's walk with the Lord was changed forever because the growth he was experiencing seemed to stop at those volatile meetings.

I was thirty-eight years old when we joined our present fellowship. Because of God's leading, my daughter experienced a very strong youth group and a godly youth leader. I have no doubt that we are where we are supposed to be. The past nine years have been absolutely wonderful in my walk with the Lord. It has been through all this that God has helped me draw closer to Him, to grow in my relationship with Him and to know what grace really means.

God knew in His infinite wisdom that unless I walked away from my cozy little life at my cozy little church that I would not understand what growing up would mean. I had to quit being a baby in Christ, I needed more than milk, I needed to get to a place in my walk where I needed meat; I needed to sink my teeth in to all I had been taught and actually apply it to myself and my walk with the Lord. I was so confused during this time of change, but I have been blessed in my new church home. The amazing walk with God that I have experienced since changing my church home has helped me see His divine intervention into my life daily. This stronger more secure walk helped me survive very difficult years. Without this growth I might have turned away from my Lord, instead of reaching out to Him even more.

> Thank you, Lord, for always leading and guiding me even in the most difficult decisions of my life. You are my counselor and my provider and I am constantly reminded of this as I look back to this change we made. So many things would not have happened if you had not brought me to this wonderful new fellowship. Thank you again for your will in my life. You know better than anyone else what is best for me and I ask that you continue to lead me in all your ways. Thank you my precious Jesus. Amen.

I have always tried through confusing moments to have a sense of humor and I often feel like my Lord has one as well because you know that there are just some situations that we get ourselves into that are just comical. I started the school year before Jeff passed away with those wonderful back to school all day meetings. The ones where you are sitting there listening to the same old thing year after year and thinking in your mind how many millions of things you could be doing in your room to get prepared for your classes. Well at this particular meeting someone from our insurance group stood up and started talking to us about some changes in the district policy. For the first time ever, they were offering open enrollment for our spouses for life insurance. I couldn't believe my ears—and I literally got tears in my eyes and chills all over when I heard this. I truly started praising God for this answer to why Jeff had laid there suffering for so long, and that he was still here so we would get a small life insurance policy for him. I went up to the lady during the next break and was very honest with her about Jeff's health and asked her if he would still qualify. She said all I needed to do was give them $10 dollars and Jeff would have a life insurance policy of $50,000 as long as he lived until October 1st.

I told so many people how God was amazing that day; now I could pay for Jeff's funeral and other outstanding debt when he passed and I just knew that was God's will. Jeff passed away on September 7. I never spoke to him about what I learned that day, he would have insisted to be put through agonizing procedures to hang on for his family but I could not let that happen. It was in God's hands; life and death and I left it at His feet. Believe me, I was and am still confused by that possibility not being fulfilled but God has other things in mind for us. My financial struggles seem to constantly multiply but that insurance was not God's answer. Sometimes we get so ahead of ourselves that we count on certain things that God does not intend for us to have. I know that through my financial struggles that God is going to use me and help me help others who need to realize that God's wonderful power can see us through anything no matter what.

> Lord, I am so grateful to you for showing me that money is not the answer. No matter how frustrating and stressful bills and debts can be, if we keep you first, we tithe first and foremost, that you will meet all of our needs. You clothe us, feed us, and support us through your grace and your people who reach out to those in need. Thank you Lord for such a family of believers who support and love their fellow Christians. Lord please take all of my confusion and help me to let it go and lean on you. On this earth we may not understand, but we need to have faith in you Lord, and understand that you know the end of the story; that our lives are truly in your hands. We are truly blessed. In Jesus' name, Amen.

FACING THE FIRE

> Blessed is the man whom God corrects; so do not despise the discipline of the Almighty.
>
> Job 5:17 NIV

What I mean by this is when I have been put in many different situations where the potter wanted to mold and shape me to His design, when I was really put to the fire. Did I stand the test or did I fail miserably and take the long road around? I know my God works all things together for good, for those who love Him but I think sometimes because of our choices the road takes several detours before we allow God to put us back on the right path. Sometimes when I was put in that hot furnace I did follow the Lord with no problem, but more times than that I failed my tests miserably. I don't like to fail tests and as a high school math teacher I know the consequences of making an F.

When we were dating, Jeff said that he had quit smoking because he knew how much I didn't like it but again I was one naive young lady. By the time I realized that Jeff had not quit I was way too involved in the relationship—I loved him so much and the wedding was in the planning stages so I didn't feel I could make it into an issue. So my first time in the furnace was when I stupidly said after we were married that every time Jeff lit a cigarette that I would too. I thought Jeff would hate the fact I was lighting up, and would smoke less and less. Instead, I got hooked on nicotine and smoked for about ten years off and on. Talk about getting burned; how ridiculous to have thought that would have worked. By the grace of God I permanently quit when I was pregnant with my son and it helped me continue to quit when I saw how difficult it was for my dad to breathe and to move from one chair to another from his fifty plus years of smoking. I definitely failed that test—I was not a witness to what God would want but jumped right in and joined the addiction.

One of the worst times in my life was after working for over five years at my first teaching position, I was given a letter in my mailbox at school telling me that I would not have a contract for the next year. For those of you who understand tenure you understand that to get a letter two days before you thought you were going to get tenure is absolutely devastating. I definitely had a faith fall at this time. How could God let this happen? I had worked so hard at doing my best. I was really involved, a pep club sponsor, cheerleading coach, always at school and always willing to help wherever it was needed, and this was how I was rewarded. I could not believe it. We had a newborn baby at home and since we had been married we had never been financially okay, and now this blow. It not only hurt me financially, but mentally as well. It is so hard to recover from being kicked in the gut without warning and to be treated unfairly.

I talked with my representative and we went to the school board and shared with them why I thought I had been unfairly treated. All I had in my file was raving reports and wonderful observations. I took letters of recommendations from men that were well respected in the community and pleaded with the board to turn over the decision and give me my job back. I later found out that the meeting lasted until 3:30 in the morning because they kept discussing my situation, however, in the end they did not change the principal's decision and I lost my job.

A lot of people out there believe that if you teach math or science that there are a million jobs out there just waiting for you, and that is just not true. That summer I applied everywhere and the ratio of applicants to openings was about 200 to 1. I just couldn't get okay with this, I struggled so much with feeling the peace and joy I should have knowing that God would take care of me but it was truly a difficult summer.

It was a few years later that I found out that my loss in my job had nothing to do with me but was the result of my new principal having a distant relative that was a math teacher. My boss had told me something verbally that last year I taught and then on paper did something that was totally the opposite. I was pregnant with my girl the year before and I had a preparation period during first hour without students. I was having an awful time with vomiting during my pregnancy and it was not only for the first three months but the entire time I was pregnant. Some days I would be on my way to work and get sick during the car ride and have to go back home to get cleaned up. I had a verbal agreement with my principal that it was okay to come in a little late as long as I got there in time for class and could teach the rest of the day. Big mistake. I should have gotten it in writing but there is that word again, naive. He had secretly been having someone in the office writing down dates and times that I was late. He did not write me up or put a disciplinary action in my file so that was why I was so blind sighted by the termination.

There were about five months of tears and confusion with all of this when God did bless me with a job in the fall. Here is where it so awesomely always works out for good, for those who love the Lord. God moved me to this new district, this district had a policy that if you worked there for two years, they would pay for your schooling to get your master's. It had to be for specific ones but if you picked one of them then it was a hundred percent free. I would have never been able to afford a master's with Jeff's unemployment history and on a teacher's salary. God worked it all out for me. I got a free master's degree in computer education. When I think of all the tears and questions I asked of the Lord during that time, I am shamed because I see now that God was always in control and his timing has always been perfect. He is the great potter and is molding us each and every day into something more like Him.

> Thank you, God, for taking care of me and blessing me more than I could have ever imagined. Please forgive me for all my doubts and fears through this time in my life. I can't believe how much energy I waste on why, what, and where in my life when all I have to do is lean on you. Thank you for saving me at this time in my life and giving me the opportunity to get a degree that later opened doors for a wonderful position. In your perfect hands I put my life, my employment, my family and my will. I again find myself unemployed Lord and ask you to guide me, direct me, and lead me to do your perfect will for my life. In Jesus' precious name, Amen.

I have spoken with three mothers who have very different stories but all of them have been dealing with challenges with their nineteen year old sons. It is so difficult to see people I care about being crushed by their children and since I was just starting challenges with my twelve year old son at the time, I can't imagine how they are dealing with their pain. I believe God has shown me these cases to let me see how important each decision and encounter I have with Jesse is and that I need to constantly be in prayer to ask God for wisdom in what I do with my son.

One mother is not a Christian and neither is her son but he is a previous student of mine. I just happened to see her walking her dog and she shared with tears in her eyes about her son. He just in the last few days had cursed her out, calling her an awful name. She discovered he had been selling drugs, as well as blatantly doing drugs in her home in front of her and she was at a total loss as to what to do. I told her that I would be praying for them, especially her son, and that the sin in this world was overwhelming to see.

The second mother is a strong Christian: she home-schooled her children and her nineteen-year-old son who never gave them any concern became a worry to her heart. He ran off with a woman who was married and had an affair with her. This strong Christian mother had to watch as her son was drawn into this web of a woman who already had five children and who was clearly going to be a stumbling block for her son. She continues still to have faith in the Lord and prays daily that her son will realize this is not God's plan for his life. She has used this time to grow closer to the Lord and lean on him in a situation that is out of her control.

The third mother was told by her son that she is an awful person. He cursed her out and left home telling her he would never have a relationship with her, and he didn't need her and he walked out of their house. This third boy buried his daddy at fifteen, and has never gotten over that tragedy. He was raised in a Christian home.

All of these women are facing the fire. All of them are being challenged by ungodliness and definite sin in their sons' lives. The only thing these women can do is pray, they can't lock their son's up in a closet, they raised them and they have to let them go but prayer is powerful and God is faithful.

My son really tried to push the envelope at the age of twelve. He wanted to "hang" with friends and just do what everyone else was doing. We definitely had a tug of war going on for a few years. I didn't know what was normal or what was due to the loss of his father. It is a very difficult place to be in. I knew though after teaching young people that to be strict is the better way to go. Once Jesse told me he was somewhere and I found out through some phone calls that he wasn't where he was supposed to be. Please check up on your children. Do not believe them when they say they are spending the night at someone's house because they work it out to lie to everyone involved and some end up walking around all night with no supervision and total freedom to sin. Anyway, I had called for Jesse and he was not where he was supposed to be so I took off in my car and drove around our small little community until I found him. He was on a corner with about thirty young people and not doing anything horrible but he was not supposed to be there. He now knows that I will call anyone, go anywhere, and that I love him enough to embarrass him in front of anyone. Jesse is now fifteen and just got his permit to drive—talk about facing the fire. I have seen my life pass before my eyes several times in the last few weeks. Jeff taught Suzie how to drive and I was not involved in that process at all. I need patience and strength to help Jesse through this wonderful time in his young life and thank God for the opportunity to have this blessing.

I am going to hang strong and ask God continually for strength and wisdom. I am going to do my best with the next few years but I don't know what the future will bring. He is a really fine young man and I am very proud of him. I still guide and direct him when I feel he is making unwise choices but I believe he knows what God wants from his life and at this time is trying to follow Him. None of us are perfect in our decisions or how we raise our children and that is why I have to believe in a sovereign God. A God that is merciful and full of grace and who loves us more than we will ever understand.

My daughter moved out on her own right after she graduated from college. She is a veterinary technician and is very good at her job. As her mother, of course, I would want her to be a Veterinarian but as Suzie says she wants to love on the animals and not be in charge. My sweet girl really has had to face the fire in those short few months that she was gone. She shared a cute little house with two roommates and was put through many tests. She basically was the only one who had a steady job and supported both of them in many ways. Through this time the Lord showed Suzie to watch out for who she should trust and how financially she was probably not ready for this move. The Lord again has taken care of us all. We have dear friends who offered to fix up half of our basement and get it ready and livable for Suzie. She was able to come back to our house and live in the basement with her own door and the freedom she needs. She is such a blessing to me and the wonderful woman she is becoming is such a testament to how faithful God is. My sweet girl is back home and helping me financially since I have lost my job and she does not have to stress about bills and responsibilities that her roommates had thrown on her.

Since my nickname is Job, I pray constantly that the Lord will bless my children and keep them safe. So many people have had to deal with children in poor health or with handicaps and I continually ask God to protect Suzie and Jesse. Job lost his children, his wealth, his livestock, and his health while undergoing the test between the Lord and the devil. I do not want that part of Job's life to become real in mine.

> Please Lord, protect and guide my children to walk with you and if it is your will, Lord, keep them safe. Lord, I just lift up these three families along with my own. Help each of them to get through these many trials. The family that is not Christians, Lord, help me to witness to them. Please be with all the mothers out there who have children who are swallowed up by sin. Help them to be strong and faithful to you. Please help me Lord to make right decisions where my children are concerned. As a single parent it gets very tiring but I know with you anything is possible. Thank you for showing us grace and mercy. In Jesus' name, Amen.

People think that if you get through the horrendous teenage years and all your poor choices children make that it becomes a much calmer situation, you have matured and won't do unwise things. I for one didn't go crazy until I was a lot older, and when I faced this fire I did not make the right choices. I failed miserably through the test the Lord provided. I was about twenty-seven years old, and I had enough of Jeff going out, and not knowing where he was, and never knowing when he would come back that I finally decided to turn the tables on him. Suzie was about one and would go to bed around eight o' clock and then I would go out with my girlfriend. She was going through an awful divorce because her husband had cheated on her and because of her devastation we decided to party three and four times a week. Jeff would be at home with Suzie and I would be out until all hours of the night. It was Jeff's turn to wonder where I was.

I look back at that time in my life and I am so ashamed at the choices I made. While we were out we had "fun," but I wasn't doing anything for God's glory and I was making a huge mistake every time we went to the bar. During this time, I continued to go to church, and was still working with the youth group, and was leading two different lives. I was drinking more than I ever had.For about fourteen months I was doing things like getting drunk and having a wild and crazy time before I was convicted to stop. I knew that all I was headed for was trouble, that I was very capable of becoming an alcoholic, and that I had to quit disappointing myself and God. I still don't get why people continue to drink to forget their problems because all they do is wake up the next day with the same problems, and with a headache, and vomiting that they didn't have before. None of those things help anyone—all they do is compound what is going on. Any type of addiction: alcohol, drugs, gambling or eating are just wrong ways of trying to cope with sin. If you are in an addiction, please give it to the Lord, and let Him take control over your wants and needs. He is all we need.

I continually seem to be in the furnace these past few years trying to deal with my husband's death, my brother's problems, and division in my family due to sin, any type of dieting, financial problems compounded, and family issues since Jeffrey's death. So many things have caused me to doubt and wonder why. I have truly said to my mother countless times: who is heartbroken because of her son's choices, who just lost a son-in-law to illness, who is losing close friends because of a family conflict, - that it is so great to give it all to the Lord. I cannot fix it, I cannot control anything, and I am not in charge, the Lord is. The knowledge that through it all He is going to take care of me; that no matter what, He loves me and that He loves my family is such a reassurance. I love Him so much!

I am so glad that my connection to the Lord doesn't depend on me and my human ways. The fact that I cannot be plucked out of His hand is so reassuring and such a wonderful consistency in a world full of sin. I love being connected to my Lord and I can't wait for that connection to continue to grow stronger. My life has so many moments where I feel the pain and pressure of being molded. It is so hard to keep my eyes on Him when I am facing those fires. However, I continually remind myself that the more I am molded, the more Christ-like I will become, and that is our goal as Christians so that others will see Jesus in our daily walk.

> Thank you, Lord, for all of my answers to prayer. Thank you for helping me in the fire times of my life and leading me on your path to righteousness. My one true goal is to become more and more like you. Help me Lord to continue to grow. In Jesus' name I pray. Amen.

REVELATIONS TO RECOVERY

> He reveals the deep things of darkness and brings deep shadows into the light.
>
> Job 12:22 NIV

In July of 2007, I found out something about Jeff that I did not know while he was alive. The news put me in kind of a tailspin. I don't know how to heal from the news since he is gone. I can't confront him. I can't express my anger. My hurt and my shock has turned inward. I have been in a self-destructing mode. I have not been successful with my diet since that time and have not been walking with the Lord as closely as I should be. I realize that this information will help me eventually but working through it has been extremely difficult. I sometimes wonder why certain things are revealed to us, and I am looking for God's purpose in allowing me to find out. That news, on top of Jeff's first birthday not being here in July, has caused deep regret in my heart.

I am trying to heal, body and soul. I focus on getting healthy, taking care of our children, seeking God's will for my life, and then someone throws a wrench into all of my plans. When we are confronted with messy things, all of us tend to react in a different way. Some of us chose to ignore it, some of us turn away from God and get angry, and some of us keep it bottled up inside and respond in ways that hurt us personally. I, at one time or another reacted in all of these ways. I was so hurt and confused that for the eight months following the revelation, it destroyed any type of success I have had with my weight and have been carrying such bitterness and anger around that the Lord couldn't bless me in the way He wanted to.

The timing of what I found out, in so many ways, was a way of protecting me, but my confusion with the Lord is why I would have to find out this information at all. But truth is very important to the Lord and I believe this had to be revealed to me in order for me to grow much more as a Christian and understand in an even greater way how much my husband, Jeff, had to be going through in his life. He had so much that he could have given the Lord but his weaknesses throughout his life kept him from the joy he could have experienced here on earth. I know that the Lord did not reveal this to me while Jeff was alive because I would not have been able to deal with this properly. I didn't find out sooner because I wouldn't have been able to face students while this was happening. I lose two teaching jobs during my career for no good reasons at all, but the Lord protects me from the one truth that could have ruined my career permanently.

I had taught high school from the very first year we were married and at the time I worried about the students coming around my house because there was not much of an age difference between us. I started teaching at the age of twenty-two and I had a senior in one of my classes who was nineteen, so being separate from my students was very important. Jeffrey had done drugs as a teenager and I was again so naive about what could happen that I turned my eyes away and did not see what was truly going on. I found out that not only was Jeff doing drugs and giving drugs to my students in my early years as a teacher, but that it continued until just a few years before his death. While I was witnessing to students, and praying for them, and inviting them to church, my husband was getting high and drunk with them.

I have felt so hurt, stupid, angry and so many more things that words cannot describe. I could have lost my job if my administration would have ever found out. Revealing this information has not only hurt me but my daughter because he was doing this with students while she was attending high school. Friends of hers were partying with her dad. Devastation describes what we are feeling to a point. How could Jeff have done this to himself, let alone his family? He knew my heart and how much I wanted the students to discover the Lord and to become Christians. How much did his habits hurt what God could have done? The Lord has revealed to me that no matter what Jeff was doing, my students still heard what I had to say, and God's word does not return void. I have to claim that promise every day and to thank the good Lord that I don't have to be responsible for what Jeff did, but for only the stupid choices I have made in my life.

No wonder Jeff had such trouble forgiving himself. There was so much deceit in our marriage. I am sure the demons he faced were why he struggled so much with loving himself. Jeff was blessed with so many things but he never seemed to get past the mistakes and decisions he had made. He never forgave himself. I know that Jeff at different times in our life asked Jesus to forgive him but he never forgave himself. Please forgive yourself and let the past go so that the Lord may use you. Grow to the point of sharing your mistakes and being bold in your witnessing. If we don't allow the good to come from the bad, how can God use it for good?

> God, help me with my bitterness and anger. Please help those who are reading my book to face things that have hurt them in their life and to let it go, Lord. In order for your will to be done in my life, I have to give all of my hurts to you and to forgive everyone. Lord, help me forgive. Lord, help me put my faith in you for why this had to happen. Lord, I lift up all of those children that were affected by Jeff and I ask you to turn that bad into good. Thank you, Lord, for revealing things to us that sometimes we don't want to see. I love you Lord.

The fact that God is still revealing the physical abuse I had as a child is another hardship that I have to recover from. To deal with these things head on will help me grow into a more positive human being. I truly believe that in order to deal with what food means to me, I have to face why it became this obsession. Slowly, I am seeing God reveal to me what a normal person uses food for. Food is beginning to be nothing to me but something I need very little of each day. When I am lonely, I need to turn to scripture. When I am scared, I need to turn on Christian music. When I am discouraged, I need to reach out to a Christian friend. Food is not what I have made it. It did not protect me back then and it is not protecting me now.

> I love you so Lord. I know that you have revealed these things to me in order for me to grow in you. I don't understand why anyone has to be abused or lied to, or why bad things happen to good people. But I do know that you are in control, and that if we have faith we will make wise choices, and will be at peace with you. Thank you, Lord, for being so close to me and for consoling me during these times of revelation. I love you. In Jesus' name, I pray. Amen.

Recovering from the death of a spouse is so difficult. God is taking me each step of the way, but I keep stumbling. Even with all of our troubles, I loved Jeff so much. He was the love of my life, and even though our marriage was no Cinderella story, we experienced many things and stuck together. Since Jeff has been gone I have felt moments of anger, grief, loneliness and just utter loss. I miss a good fight every once in a while. I miss looking at his smile and wish that things could have been better. I mourn what our marriage could have been. I know that we did what we did, and made the choices we made, but you always do the "what ifs". Each day I ask the Lord to help me have more joy and peace than the day before.

I realize that all of us have experienced loss and God chooses different ways to reveal things to us to help us heal. Please look for people who have suffered devastating things but have chosen to lean on the Lord instead of running away. Be a testament to what God can do. Recovery from suffering is an individual thing. It is between God and you. Help yourself by letting the Lord reveal to you the truths you need to face in order to recover. I know that there is no greater help for me than the Lord's help. I have good and bad days; at the end of each of them I thank the Lord for everything and all of the blessings I have received.

> Lord, I know that I have so much more to learn. I know that each and everything you choose to reveal to me is going to help my walk with you. Lord, I ask you to be with all of the people who are going through struggles they don't understand. Help them to choose you. I can't imagine going through anything without you. Thanks for your infinite wisdom and timing in revealing things to me. I love you. In Jesus' name, I pray. Amen.

GENERATED BY GRACE

> My intercessor is my friend as my eyes pour out tears to God; on behalf of a man he pleads with God as a man pleads for his friend.
>
> Job 16: 20, 21 NIV

I think I was about thirty-six years old when I really got the whole grace thing. When I really understood what God's grace had done for me. I can't believe it took me that long, especially being raised in a Christian home and being a Christian since I was ten, but I am so thankful that I finally got it. God showed me in His infinite wisdom how wonderful it was to have grace given to you, and how great it felt to give someone else grace.

Godly
Response
Against
Conceivable
Evil

I had forgiven people for doing things to me before, and was never one to hold grudges, well at least not too long, but to actually give someone grace is something I am still learning. To give someone all you have, all the love you can give when it is undeserved. That's what I believe grace is in my life. God continues to give me grace daily for where I fail Him, but His ultimate example of grace was when He gave His one and only Son for our sins. How unworthy I am for such a sacrifice.

So many people, Christian friends, were telling me to leave Jeff and get a divorce. If you are familiar with the book of Job then you know how Job's three friends try to give him advice. They try to convince him that if he just would repent of what he had done, the awful things that were happening to him would stop. Job tried to tell them that he had done nothing to repent of (I wish I could say that) and that God would take care of him. God allowed these things to happen. It was not to punish or ruin Job but to let Satan see that no matter what he did to Job: Job would stand the test. There have been many challenges in my life that I did not stand the test as wisely as Job, but I am a work in progress, and I know that the Lord isn't finished with me yet. I do have one strong Christian friend, actually my closest friend that will speak truth to me. God's truth whether I want to hear it or not. Through much prayer and her wise counsel God helped me continue to stay in my marriage no matter what the challenge was at the time.

I was on a mission trip when God spoke to me so clearly that I had to quit thinking divorce was an option, I had to quit looking for the answers to all that had happened, and just lean on Him. Prayer and more prayer would see me through the rest of my marriage and I just had to continue to trust in the Lord to take care of us.

I could not continue if I had to be perfect to get to heaven. To get through the day and know that God forgives and shows me grace is such an amazing relief. We need to show others grace like God continually shows us. Why do we most of the time become these unforgiving people who don't let people forget what they have done to us? I have been crushed emotionally by quite a few people in my lifetime and if I wouldn't have let that go, if I wouldn't forgive them how can I expect the Lord to forgive me?

Please, give the Lord anything keeping you from a stronger relationship with Him. This doesn't mean you are going to be perfect, but it does mean that you do know what you need to do. That you understand that God would have you show others grace whenever you can, so that they can understand God's grace for us as sinners. We have to be that example that shows the world that we are different, that even though we are human, we handle situations different and that we have Christ in our hearts. As you encounter people at work and just in your daily routines, before you respond, think about what God would do. Recently, when the superintendent told me I was being terminated and that I was done that day was a really could example of how God helped me think before I spoke because at that moment I would not have responded in a Christ-like manner. I couldn't go back to my room, I couldn't say goodbye to my friends or students; I was just plucked from the building. I know that it was God who kept my temper in place and that it was God who helped me stay calm and not say what my flesh wanted to say. I am still working on forgiveness to those who spied on me, and helped the men in power to release me but I know that I believe in God's grace and that I have to give it to these people if I am to go on. Those WWJD bracelets really are the right idea and shouldn't be worn flippantly. Instead, they should be worn with the actual desire to do what Jesus would do.

The grace that God shows me daily is so awesome. When my children do something that just cuts at my heart, which hurts to my very core, it breaks me more than anyone else possibly could. When others attack us or hurt us it is nothing to what your child can do, and as parents we suffer. As I think about this and relate it to me being a child of God, I can't believe how much I have hurt my Lord. I look around at spiritual people, and the flagrant sin that they are committing, and the constant stumbling I do; I can't imagine the pain we have caused God. We need to understand that our relationship with the Lord is number one, that what we do each moment either blesses Him or curses Him. We need to realize that He is right here, and listening, and feeling every moment of our lives, and that as our Father, we need to love and respect Him. We should not abuse Him because we know He will show us grace, we should embrace Him more because of His love.

> Grace, grace, God's grace. Grace that is greater than all our sin. Grace, grace, God's grace. Grace that will pardon and cleanse within. Grace, grace, God's grace. Grace that is greater than all our sin.
> "Grace That is Greater Than All Our Sin",
> The Baptist hymnal

Music means almost as much to me in my spiritual walk as the words of a sermon. The wonderful way that people have put words to a great melody is so comforting to me. All of the old hymns that I was raised with, all the new praise songs I hear at youth camps, and all of the solos that are performed just bless my soul. Being raised with a pianist has taught me all music has its place and the kind that lifts up my Lord is all that I want to be surrounded by. My mom has written so many beautiful songs and has always used her talent for God's glory. I wish that she had persisted in getting them published because I know that each of them could be a blessing to others. Singing songs that talk about grace, peace, and just the joy that my relationship with the Lord brings is what I want to be immersed in.

Sometimes it is so hard to show this kind of grace to other people. There are so many people who have hurt me through the years, making fun of my size, being cruel at work because of their jealousy of how the kids love me, and those family and friends that don't agree with how or what I believe was best for Jeff. I continually try to have God's grace toward these people because I remember the scripture that says if I don't forgive them, why should Christ forgive me? My willingness to let God help me forgive is why Jeffrey and I stayed together through it all and why I have been able to forgive deep hurts. Forgiveness is the least I can do since Jesus has forgiven me for so much. I cannot stand in judgment of anyone around me because we are all doing the best we can.

Unless you have walked in exactly the same shoes as someone, then you can't say what they are doing is wrong or against what God would have them do. I have shared with friends when I thought they were doing something totally against what the Bible tells us to do. I have not judged them but have tried to share what I believe scripture has to say on the subject. I have lost friends over standing up for what the Bible says, and have had to make choices to stand by the truth in my life when it was very difficult to do. We have to use the Bible to guide us in our lives and our decision making or we don't truly love the Lord or respect his authority. Think about your closest friends and family and how often you ask their advice, we need to accept God's counsel with everyday issues and realize His will and sovereign power that we can receive. If we want His blessings on our life we must use His word to guide us daily.

We were so blessed to have Jeff's mother help us through the last two and a half years of his life. Before Jeff went into the hospital his mom stayed with us for a year and a half Monday through Friday so I could continue to work and carry the medical insurance we so desperately needed. She not only took care of Jeff but helped around the house and cooked us dinner; it was wonderful. We have a fairly small house and five people with one bathroom was a challenge, but definitely worth it. I will never be able to thank her enough for choosing to help us. I know that Jeff was alive for a longer time because of her care.

When Jeff was in the hospital and receiving twenty-four hour care, she still continued to stay with him from early morning to late at night. The love and care she showed her youngest son was amazing. Her husband lived an hour and a half away and she rarely saw him. Her chosen sacrifice was full of love and grace that only a mother can give. What an awesome testimony she had to sacrifice her life for her son.

Because of our two children, and a full time job, and my failing health I couldn't give Jeff the same amount of time as his mom. I think there were times when Jeff didn't understand, but I truly believe that I did the best I could during those years. In the end, the fact that our time together was good, and we were not fighting, but reading the Bible was such an awesome example of God's grace.

If you have not shown God's grace to someone lately, please take the time right now to ask God to give you the strength it takes to do just that. A friend or a family member who you have not forgiven. Life is too short for us to cling to things that don't matter. Please find the peace that passes all understanding when you let go of un-forgiveness and all of that anger. Your life will be so much better. You will feel the peace immediately.

Jesus showed us how to do it when he forgave those at the foot of the cross. Don't let His witness be in vain; use His example to do what you need to do.

> Lord, I just ask you to help all of us to show your grace to others. Please help me to forgive those who don't show me grace, and to let their judgments not affect my life, and what you would do with it. Convict us of people we have problems with Lord and help us give it over to you. In Jesus' precious gracious name, Amen.

SHELLS BY THE SEASIDE

> He marks out the horizon on the face of the waters
> for a boundary between light and darkness.
>
> Job 26:10 NIV

It is so comforting for me to realize how close Jesus is to me, minute by minute. I think that some people feel a little nervous by this fact but I guess that I am so needy for His magnificent arms around me that I just sit back and enjoy the warmth and comfort He provides. I am so tired from years of struggle and confusion that to just let Him have complete control is such a relief that I can finally enjoy everything. This story I am about to share is probably one where you had to be there to actually sense the full picture, but it was so powerful to me that I want to share, and just ask you to imagine walking along side of me on the beach.

I was given an opportunity to travel when school was out, June of 2007, for two weeks without my children. At the time my daughter, Suzie was twenty, and my son, Jesse was thirteen and I know it was selfish but was a much needed break. I needed that time so I could come back refreshed and a much better mother. At least that is what I try to convince myself when I do these selfish things. Anyway, I was able to take a road trip to Hilton Head, South Carolina with one of my dearest friends, Lori, for a glorious two weeks and enjoy God's majestic ocean.

It was our last day on the beach and it is hard to explain my passion for just how close I feel to the Lord walking along the seaside: praising Him, talking to Him, singing to Him and just feeling so close to His awesome power and divine grace that there is no place I would rather be. The women I was with on this trip I think felt a little insulted, because I didn't want to sit and visit while we were on the beach. I wanted to walk and talk with my Savior. Don't get me wrong, I walk and talk with Him everywhere, but the feeling of eternity and everlasting power comes much easier to me on the ocean. I know that I am destined to retire to a beach community and just feel this wonder daily.

I was walking by myself singing praise songs and enjoying the absolutely gorgeous day with clear blue skies and a gentle breeze. I had collected just very small shells throughout the week, and if you have ever been to Hilton Head you know that it is not a beach known for a lot of shells, but there had been quite a few storms that month, and there were more shells than I had seen there in a few years. As I was walking, I came across a little girl about seven years old with a bucket of shells, huge conk shells that were beautiful and several other unusual shells, so I struck up a conversation with her.

She told me that her daddy had found them for her, and as we were talking her father came up to join us. He tried to explain to me how to watch the tide and figure out just the right time to grab a shell from the sand, and the ocean, and that he had gotten quite good at it because he had three daughters who all wanted pretty shells. This was the day before Father's Day and having buried my daddy seven years ago, and also being very sentimental about my children having to experience their first Father's Day without Jeffrey, it was a very emotional day. Also, my sweet brother-in-law, Rodney, just three days before, buried his dad of a sudden illness all caused me to be an even more sentimental fool about daddies. Because of all of these feelings, I told the sweet little girl that she had a very special dad it seemed, and did she know what tomorrow was? She looked a little puzzled so I reminded her it was Father's Day and that she needed to treat him special.

After leaving this conversation, I was not only an emotional mess but I also shared with the Lord how much I would love a beautiful conk shell. I was leaving the next day and would love to take one home as a souvenir. It was about fifteen feet after that conversation with the little girl and her daddy that I looked up and there was the most perfect conk shell I had ever seen just laying on the beach right in front of me. I didn't have to do anything that the man had told me to do about the sand and the tide, it was right there in front of me. I got goose bumps, and felt like the Lord just plopped a shell right in front of me to gather in my arms and have as a souvenir.

You must understand there were several people walking along the beach, the father and daughter I had just talked to had come from this direction so why and how had no one picked this shell up if it was there? I believe with all my heart that it was placed there, revealed just for me and was a precious reminder of how much God wants to give us the desires of our heart. I realized that I have much greater desires that have not been answered yet but God was letting me know that He does hear, that He does care, and that He does respond.

Unbelievably, I kept walking that day and received three conk shells bigger than my fist, and several other large perfect shells. He not only gave me one but He blessed me over and abundantly of what I had asked. God will always do that for us if we are obedient to Him, and believe that He will answer us. Psalms 20:4 says, “May he give you the desire of your heart and make all your plans succeed.” Have you had a seaside experience?

Without the assurance that anything is possible in Christ you will constantly limit what God wants to do in your life. Please let Him in and let Him have full reign and power with your daily walk. It doesn’t have to be on the seaside but it can be that powerful and immediate anywhere if we just let Him.

> Lord, thank you so much for that moment in time when I felt your presence right there offering me those beautiful shells. Help me to remember how close you are and that you want to be called on, minute by minute. Lord, thank you for the rela-

> tionship I have with you and for the opportunity to see your glory in the ocean and the sand. I love you so much and continually pray for more shells that you want to give me. Thank you for how wonderful you are to me and how much you supply all of my needs. Amen.

It had been months since I had been to the beach since this experience and again God blessed me with a word from Him. I was able to get away on President's weekend and go to the beach and get a few days away from the insanity of high school and all that it can bring. As I was walking, and praying with the Lord, I was looking for those perfect shells on the beach when I suddenly felt the Lord revealing to me that, as people and as Christians, we are like the shells on the beach. None of them are perfect. I know. I know this isn't a stunning fact for most of us. We are not perfect and we never will be.

Jesus Christ was the only perfect being in this world. We, as Christians, are supposed to strive to be like Christ but we also need to realize that perfectionism can also be a stumbling block with our walk with Him. I started to pick up broken shells for all the things that I need to be broken of. My addiction to food, my loneliness, my anger with my administration at my previous job, my children and my lack of doing God's will in my life. Each of these shells, these five things, God lay on my heart on the seashore. I have so many issues but these were the ones revealed to me that day. Anytime I face one of these five things, I look at those broken shells and realize that only with God's help will I be unbroken. He has taken away my frustration with my administration by terminating my time at that school. He has blessed me with two good kids and I know that I am not a perfect parent but through my brokenness He is revealed in their lives. My weight and loneliness are still being made whole but I am definitely trying to daily give God my life. I want to walk in His will and write this book, speak for His kingdom and even with my cracks and broken pieces God will carry me through.

Again, I walk with the Lord daily and I don't have to be at the beach to do that. The time I do spend there is definitely quality time, like the hunter who likes to just go out in the woods for the tranquility and not the kill, or like the fisherman who just wants to sit in his boat all day long and not get frustrated when he doesn't catch anything. All of us have those spots where refreshing reflective thoughts can and do happen. In order for the potter to mold us in His image, we have to become broken so that He can shape us into what He designed for our life.

I brought those five broken shells home, and have them on my dresser, and when I look at them I pray about each of those struggles in my life, and give them to the Lord. I am so hard headed and stubborn with these issues that I just thank the good Lord for His mercy and grace.

> Lord, continue to break me so that I can be more like you. Remind me, Lord, of your direction in my life so that I can keep my eye on the prize and run a good race. I have so many things that

> are distracting, and I need to remember that being your servant and disciple is what I am here for. Lord, guide me, direct me, and bring me more revelations like when I am walking on the beach. I love you, Lord.

The Lord, again, blessed me with a special "seashell." I had been so discouraged with my job situation and was crying out to Him each day for direction. Should I try to teach again? Should I try to do ... I had no idea what I should do. Family and friends had always been so wonderful and supportive but what would I do if a job didn't come along? I was a widow with two children and all I had ever done was teach. I knew God had called me to this profession, but wondered whether he was guiding me into a different direction. I would love to travel and speak to women, and young people, and share with them how glorious God is, but would that happen overnight? I wanted my book to be published but who would I choose to do that? Should I self-publish? Should I spend $3,000 I don't have to get it published? You are probably wondering where the seashell is in all this confusion.

I received a phone call from a student who had graduated two years ago and he wanted to write a human interest paper about me for a class at college. I thought that was really sweet and had no idea what he would write but we met and talked for almost two hours. It was nice to have that time remembering what he thought about his class with me. I feel like this was a seashell just for me from the Lord because he wrote about me and it touched my heart so much; the timing was perfect. I needed a touch from God about whether I should continue to teach, and I believe this paper was my answer. I would like you to read it because Collin summarizes who I am very succinctly and since you have now heard how I lost two jobs, I would like you to see who I am through the eyes of a previous student. This is not about my pride, but it is about how God uses certain people to answer questions or encourage us right when we need it. Here is what was written:

What do you do when your nickname is Job? This is the biblical reference that Jane Sneed, forty-seven, has chosen as the title of her book. Until the winter of 2008, Jane Sneed taught math at Brentwood High School for over thirteen years, over half of her twenty-four years of teaching experience.

Sneed has a sunny disposition, smiling and giggling away, despite the rough times.

"I try to work with whatever God blesses me with," says Sneed, smiling as she stirs a low-fat yogurt parfait and hums quietly to herself.

Sneed's husband, Jeff, passed away in September of 2006 after a long battle with complications due to diabetes.

"He was bedridden for the last six months of his life," Sneed said, "it was very hard. There were nights that I'd stay in the hospital all night with him, shower there and go straight to class in the morning to teach."

Calmly battling tears, Sneed is unemployed now, and is working to make life better. After meeting with the Superintendent of the school district, Jane Sneed officially resigned for personal reasons. Due to legal issues, Sneed can't speak openly about her resignation without risking losing her considerable severance package for the school.

"I've got nine months of pay," says Sneed, "so you might be able to look at it as a really long paid vacation [laughs] but in September it stops, so I need to find some work. People have told me I should get away from teaching, but what else would I do? I love it more than anything."

Twenty-three years of teaching and her students love her. The day after Sneed "resigned" from the district, just a week before Christmas Day, over fifty students marched out of the school in protest.

"Bless them, they called Channel two and Channel five, they really fought for me," says Sneed.

A Facebook group, "Petition to Support Jane Sneed," sprung up almost overnight. Two hundred and ninety-one students of Sneed's belong to the group, and it contains over 40 testimonials of students who valued her as a teacher. The group, which officially petitioned to the district, is a fine example of Mrs. Sneed's impact on students.

One parent of a former student claims that Mrs. Sneed is the only teacher who had the patience to deal with his sons attention deficit disorder. "Thank you, Jane Sneed. Our family loves you."

Sneed's son, Jesse, is a freshman at the school, and can find himself uncomfortable attending the school his mother was employed with for so long.

"I know he feels uncomfortable sometimes, he doesn't like going into the office, it has got to be tough on him," Sneed says in a somber, low voice.

Sipping on diet coke with lemon wedges, and cheerful all the while, Sneed misses the students the most. Her former classroom at the school was a testament to her devotion. The white brick walls, so stark in their plainness, were decorated with hundreds of pictures of former students over the years, lining the whole room.

"It took about 5 hours to take them (the pictures) down. I still have them in my room, but I can't look at them much right now, it makes me too sad to see all their faces," says Sneed.

Sneed's daughter and oldest child, Suzanne Sneed, 21, recently moved back home to live with her mother and brother, to contribute her own paychecks in the tough times. The Sneed's are also a deeply religious family. Jeff and Jane met in high school through their church and dated all the way through college before marrying.

"We were told we might have trouble conceiving children, but I wanted as many as possible," says Sneed. "After Suzanne, I had a tubal pregnancy. It nearly killed me, and I only had one (fallopian) tube left, which meant it'd be very hard to have another child. Jesse was a blessing, a gift from the Lord."

One could argue though, that Mrs. Jane Sneed has hundreds of children.

Her 300 children gathered in the auditorium in 2005 to shout into a video camera, "ABC, GIVE MRS. SNEED A HOUSE!" in a video submission to the popular show, Extreme Home Makeover.

Her children, dozens of them, used to eat lunch in her classroom every day, bringing her McDonald's Monopoly game pieces so that she could "hit the jackpot." Her children marched out of school in protest.

Her children called her the night she left school forever, some of them crying, offering help, love, and support.

Her children, over forty of them, left school on the day of her husband's funeral, piled into her church, just to show that they cared.

One of her children spoke at the funeral, a student, just to tell her that he cared.

Her children formed a caravan of cars, and joined the funeral procession to Jeff Sneed's grave, gathering around his coffin, grieving with their math teacher, mother and friend.

Her current work, a part time teaching job at a learning center, doesn't pay the bills well.

"It's work, and it's teaching, and it's what I have right now," said Sneed.

Her book reflects her struggle, her faith, and her message to future generations.

"It's easy to just stay in bed, to not get up, and carry on every day. It's been hard before, but you have to. I still consider myself a lucky person, I've been blessed. I run into former students, (laughing) my family jokes that they can't take me anywhere without running into someone who used to be a student. It reminds me why I teach, and why I love it."

Her children will miss her.

I love the way Collin wrote about my "children." He knew from experience that that was the way I thought of my students. He will probably never understand the joy this paper gave me. I was deeply struggling with what I should do, and God used him to possibly answer that question. My life is in the Lord's hands and I am not sure where I am headed but this paper made me feel like teaching is still a definite option.

The gift and the 'seashell' of this whole experience is that Collin is a young man that I tried to witness to during his two years in my classes. We had several discussions about faith and what it means, and Collin is a professed atheist. Would you have ever thought someone who did not believe in God wrote that paper? I know that God is still using me and the words I spoke to all of my students are still in their heads. God used this to touch my life and lift me up. I did not solicit these wonderful words but God used this young man to let me hear them.

> Lord, thank you so much for these words. I love teaching and I love you. Help me to use both to help others, God. I want to witness and reach out to those in need. I want students who don't necessarily believe what I do to still respect me enough to accept who I am. Help my witness during times of struggle, Lord, to be pleasing to you. I lift up all of my prior students, Lord, who don't know you, and I ask you to send someone to them that will continue what you and I started. I love you so much. In Jesus' name. Amen.

WALKING ON WATER

> He performs wonders that cannot be fathomed,
> miracles that cannot be counted.
>
> Job 9:10 NIV

How awesome it would have been to be there and see Jesus walk on the water, to witness that wonderful miracle on that day. But what I love about my relationship with the Lord is that He has taught me that each day is a miracle. Seeing the sunset and the beautiful colors of the sky, waking up to the birds and the trees, and knowing without a doubt that my God, my Savior, created them all is a miracle.

The most vivid miracles in my life have been the births of our two children. People who have ever been around a baby and held that precious life in their arms should not ever doubt that there is a God. The process of the pregnancy didn't just suddenly happen. The intricate parts of the developing of the fetus show how much God cares and how much He is in control.

When I got pregnant with Suzie, we were so excited

and couldn't believe we were going to have a baby. We hadn't been expecting it because I was told I might need help to conceive, but we had our own little miracle growing inside of me. The morning sickness that is only supposed to last for three months and only be in the morning was definitely not the case during my pregnancy. I threw up constantly, morning, noon and night. It was helpful with my size because during the whole nine months I only gained eighteen pounds. My diet was basically crackers and even the day I was in labor I threw up four times.

As I said all pregnancies are miracles but Suzie was definitely a special blessing. Her due date was May 21, which was perfect because then I would be able to spend the whole summer with my new baby before going back to work in the fall. I was so excited and happy and scared all at the same time. I was almost twenty-six years old and the overwhelming responsibility of it all was terrifying. I knew that God would help me and guide me, but I couldn't believe it was about to happen.

During the last month of my pregnancy, when I had three different showers, I was way too sick to enjoy any of them. I remember one in particular that I was told was for my friend, Gail, and the morning of the shower I called my mom and said that I had a fever and really felt awful. I didn't think I was going to be able to make it. That's when my mom had to break down and tell me that it was for me and I was going. We found out later that day that my fever was 102 degrees and I was very sick. It was the third of May and I went to sleep that night knowing that I would probably have to call my doctor on Monday because of how I was feeling. I didn't make it until Monday; I was at the hospital that very night. My dad drove me to the hospital in the middle of the night because Jeff wouldn't wake up and help me. He thought I was blowing things out of proportion about how I felt and he needed sleep for the job he had at that time. I couldn't believe it when they diagnosed pneumonia and admitted me so that they could keep an eye on the baby. They assured me everything was going to be okay and not to worry about the baby but I was so scared not knowing what was going to happen.

I was there until Friday the eighth of May after being on an I.V. of antibiotics. I was so tired and ready to rest for the few weeks I had until the due date. However the next night, the ninth of May, my water broke and Jeff and I left that morning on the tenth for the hospital. We waited quite a while before we left because Jeff didn't believe that my water broke, he just thought I was having bladder problems as I had throughout the pregnancy. I couldn't believe I was in labor, on May 10, 1987 on Mother's Day. I was going to become a mother on Mother's Day, how exciting that was.

I went through eighteen hours of labor after having pneumonia; I was beyond weak and couldn't even breathe through my contractions. My husband was sitting in a recliner watching the Cardinals play a baseball game and teased with my doctor about naming our child Jose Aquendo or Jack Clark. All I did was lie on my side and squeeze Jeff's hand until he had a bruise the size of St. Louis. We had about twenty five people in the waiting room for the news, people praying everywhere because of my weight, my pneumonia, and the fact that Suzie was early were all concerns we had. Right before I began pushing the doctor took Jeff out in the hall and let him know how serious the situation could become. My doctor was worried about me making it through, I didn't know that until later, but God worked all things out that day for good. "Come to me all who are weary and I will give you rest," and that's exactly what He did.

At 6:16 p.m. our beautiful Suzanne Marie was born. She had trouble breathing at first and was rushed to the I.C.U. because of the pneumonia I had. She had to be put on an antibiotic right away to ward off any problems. She had to have an I.V. in her forehead while she was in the hospital; the doctor said that was the safest place for it. When my doctor held her up he said, "Say hello to your little miracle," I was in such awe of her. Each detail of her precious face, the dimples in her elbows and that she had curly red hair held my gaze for months to come. We both stayed in the hospital for five days because of everything we had endured and I was taken home with my sweet baby. I was still recovering so my sisters both helped with her care while Jeff was at work and she was loved on by so many. His mother also flew in from California to see her first grandbaby and stayed four weeks to help me through my sicknesses.

I had been home about nine days when I started having another fever and my back was in such pain that we had to call an ambulance. I was so upset about leaving Suzie and having to go back to the hospital that I withdrew into myself. I didn't want visitors and I didn't want anything but my baby. I was, again, admitted but this time it was a urinary tract infection that was affecting my kidneys. I had been there two days when Jeff surprised me with bringing Suzie to the front lobby. He didn't want her to come to the room because of the germs but I got to hold her for about an hour. That meant so much to me that he actually thought about it. I got to be with my baby and feel her in my arms again.

God was so alive in our lives at this time. I was in constant prayer over our daughter and my health. He let me feel His presence daily and I knew without Him I wouldn't have made it. I was so weak and tired from being sick but when I got home that time I was able to stay with my girl until the fall. We actually got to go to the beach when she was about two-and-a-half months old, and I got to be at my favorite place with my favorite miracle.

It was almost seven years before our second miracle was born. This one even more surprising because Jeff had diabetes now and I had lost a tube. With lower sperm and one less tube God blessed us with Jesse. Both of our children are named after people we love because that was important to both of us. We wanted to let people know how much we thought of them and because of that Suzanne Marie is named for my sister Sue, my mom Jean Suzanne, and Jeff's mom RoseMarie, and Jesse Richard was named after my daddy Jesse, Jeff's dad George Richard and Jeff's stepdad, Richard. So I think with just two children we have hit very special people in our lives. My pregnancy with Jesse was different than Suzie's in a lot of ways but there was still trouble due to health problems.

I threw up with Jesse for the first few months but not as often and not as much. We had to deal with something much more serious towards the last two months of the pregnancy. I was having a gestational pregnancy, a diabetic one, and my doctor was so concerned about the baby's size. He wanted to take the baby as early as possible but wouldn't until the lungs were fully developed. During the last two months I had to give myself three shots of insulin a day, because of the diabetes, and I was told then that in a few years I would probably have the disease because of this pregnancy. All of these things factored in to me having to have three amniocentesis to check Jesse's lungs, and going to the doctor every day for the last month to be hooked up to a heart monitor to make sure Jesse was okay. In the end, we couldn't take Jesse early because of his lungs but because of his ten pounds, ten ounces we had to schedule a c-section for January 28, 1994.

He was such a big, healthy looking baby and this time my doctor jokingly said when he held him up that this baby was ready to walk. Because of the diabetes, however, he had to also be put in I.C.U. for a few days to be monitored. He looked so funny with all those itty bitty babies but he was still being watched as closely as them because he had a rough entrance to the world.

I couldn't believe we had two such beautiful miracles in our lives. How God blessed us twice. I believe we both would have had more children but with Jeff's health and my difficult pregnancies, it was not going to happen. I love babies, I love to hold babies and they seem to love me. I tell everyone that I am like a wonderful soft water bed to them and all babies want to do is lie on my tummy and fall asleep. They lie on my chest and typically fall asleep rather quickly even if they don't know me too well. I would like to one day volunteer at a hospital and hold sick babies because it is something I feel God would like me to do. I can't believe after going to hospitals so much with my husband that I would consider going on a volunteer basis but I know that there would be joy in helping those precious miracles. Hopefully one day.

> Lord, thank you so much for my precious miracles. I know daily that I receive miracles but the two lives that you have given me to watch over for you, Lord, are just wonderful. Thank you for all the miracles of life and just daily for taking the time to show me more things that come from you. In Jesus' precious name. Amen.

HEAVEN IS MY HOME

> Even now my witness is in heaven; my advocate is on high.
>
> Job 16:19 NIV

In the past ten years, I have realized that we have got to be set apart, that we have got to stand out, that it is okay to be considered weird—we are not of this world. I am so thankful that I am ready at anytime to go home, to my true home, with my Lord and Savior. I have total peace that whenever that day may come that I am ready. Don't get me wrong, I want to see my children grow up, and all that but I know that whenever that day is, God is in control and that His timing is perfect.

I used to love to read romance novels on the beach, watch movies at the theatre, sit at a restaurant with friends who weren't Christians, but now I can say that those situations make me uncomfortable. I don't want to read about two people having a romance who are not married, I don't want to be embarrassed about what is on the movie screen, and I shouldn't feel alright sitting around while people are cursing or drinking, and be okay with it. In my life, there have been times when I did do these things. Those friends of mine out there reading this are wondering when this all happened because they have seen me do these things; please believe me when I say that they are happening less often now and that each time God helps me realize it was a bigger mistake than before.

As human beings we continue to do things over and over again that displease God. It is because the devil knows our weaknesses, and is very good at bringing them up in our times of struggle. This is why each day, each moment, we must cry out to God and ask Him to guide us right then, that very moment, so we can resist the things of this earth. I feel so much better when I am walking with the Lord, minute by minute. When I am only listening to Christian music in my car, and watching things on television that are pleasing to the Lord. We should stand up for what is moral and ethical and not be ashamed of being a Christian. I absolutely get goose bumps when I listen to Carmen singing "We Need God in America Again." That is exactly how as people striving to be holy should feel. We should stand firm on our biblical beliefs, and be proud of our Lord and Savior Jesus Christ.

There are three places where I feel like I am in heaven. First, is when I am in my church worshiping and singing praise songs with my girl on one side and my son on the other, and we are just praising the Lord, we aren't fighting over silly things like we do at home but we put all that junk aside, and stand there knowing how wonderful it is to have a personal relationship with Jesus. Now, because our ages are fifteen, twenty-one and forty-seven those walks are a bit different but the one thing, the most important thing is that we have Jesus in our hearts and we know one day we will live in heaven for eternity. Second, is sitting on the beach looking at the waves and being reminded of how majestic God is. I sit and sing praise songs and just pray continuously as I remember how mighty my God is, and that He can conquer any problem or dissolve any burden that I may have. For those times when I can't get to an ocean, living in the mid-west, the next best thing is driving around in my convertible at night with the stars as my ceiling and listening to praise songs, which is my third heavenly spot. I would love to sound like Sandi Patty but unlike her I just try to sing and love belting out whatever notes those are. With the stars as my stage and no one listening I worship like there is no tomorrow. It feels so good to be there, right there just me and my Father in heaven. Those moments are why I know that this is not my home.

My third heavenly place, my convertible, was taken away from me. I guess I was belting out some bad notes so the universe decided to get me away from my car. Two months after I lost my job, I went to a job fair about twenty miles from my house. I was so excited and just knew that I would come away from the fair with a job for the fall. Big mistake! There were two thousand unemployed teachers in a room the size of a small box. I was so upset and depressed by so many people needing jobs that I left fairly early. On my way home, on the highway, my sweet red convertible decided to break down. I barely got off the highway when it came to a total stop. I realize to feel such a bond with a thing is silly but the Lord and I had spent a lot of time together in that car. It lost its transmission that day and I had to realize that I could not pay to repair it. My convertible was gone. Again, God blesses me in so many ways. My sister decided to sell me her daughter's car for $2,000, even though it was worth much more. That was such a blessing and then God even topped that because my other sister and her husband decided to bless me by paying the $2,000 for me. I know I am still the spoiled baby of the family and blessed by my amazing sisters.

I would like to share at this point one of the coolest things that has happened to me in twenty-three years of teaching. In the spring of 2006, a senior at my high school, who was in my advisory came to me and said that he along with the rest of the seniors were going to nominate me and my family for an extreme home makeover. I said, wow that would be great but really didn't think they would go through with it but I underestimated Nathan and how motivated he was to try and bless me. Nathan is a young man who I asked to help me a few times at my home with heavy things, or difficult projects that my husband being so sick couldn't possibly do. He helped with the yard, moved furniture, fixed our computers and just was always willing and never would accept anything but a thank you. He is such a fine young man.

Anyway, he decided that we were in pretty bad shape and that with all we had been through that we were a shoe-in for the show. He taped all four of us, Jeff had been in the hospital thirty days at that point and so Nathan had to go there to interview him, he also got the principal on board and at a school wide assembly the kids stood behind me and on the count of 3 said, please ABC give Ms. Sneed a new house . It was so amazing to hear almost 300 students scream that and that they supported me and cared enough to be a part of it. I love my students and they will never understand how much that meant to me. I never heard from ABC, but hearing those children that day already made me a winner. My home that I have is a blessing and even though there are needed repairs we are blessed to have one and I know that if ABC doesn't call there was someone else who needed a home more.

My home is such a blessing and I am so happy where I am. I live a mile from where I worked at the time and my children were able to go to a wonderful school right in our neighborhood. It doesn't matter if the paint is chipping as long as the love is there. I want my children to feel comfortable and loved. I want Christ in the center of this house and our hearts. We have been blessed with a home here on earth and all of us know that our heavenly home awaits us. Heaven is becoming more and more wonderful as my loved ones go on before me; my husband, my daddy, my grandma and grandpa, my uncle, and dear friends that I can't wait to spend eternity with them praising the Lord. Oh, what a marvelous day that will be when Jesus my Savior I see, and I can only imagine what it will be like to walk in His sight. Lord, thank you for saving me and making a place for me. If all I can do in return is spread your good news and be a witness to your glory, that isn't any sacrifice at all but a joy unspeakable.

Your heaven on earth may be several different places or one special place. It doesn't matter as long as you are meeting Jesus there. Take time to come to this place daily, to spend time in the word, to sing praises, to experience God's overwhelming spirit over you when you and Him are in that wonderful quiet place where such peace and joy is restored and supplied for all your needs.

> Lord, again, I just want to thank you for bringing me to this place in my walk that I feel your presence so easily. Lord, continue to guide me and help me to follow you. I pray that, as Christians, we will truly understand that we need to be set apart and that we are not afraid to be condemned or persecuted for you. Thank you for providing Jesus so that heaven is there for us, for eternity with you. Love and praise to your holy name, Amen.

CONCLUSION

I pray that something in these pages has helped you with your walk in this life. We all have struggles, temptations and trials, and I truly pray that whatever God has had me share has touched you right where you are. I am far from perfect, and I am a sinner like all of us but the thing I hope has happened with this attempt of my writing is that God has used my difficulties to help you. God can use anything or anyone to trigger something in your life to cause you to grow with Him if you choose to. Don't ever give up, lean on our Lord and you will feel a peace that surpasses anything this world can offer.

I am not real sure how long it is supposed to take to write a book or how long an official book would be but I believe I have covered everything God has wanted me to at this time. There are so many other things in my life that I could share but I don't want to bore you on my first try. There are so many blessings that I have not shared but every trial has been a blessing because each tribulation brought me closer to the Lord. If you do not agree with anything in this book please do agree on one thing: God is Faithful!

I cannot believe the healing that has come from my heart while writing this book; how God has just helped me face each thing and to again make sure I have His heart as I deal with each one. I can't believe it has taken me this long to obey, this long to respond to His call after feeling so much relief by doing it. Please don't waste time, please recognize God's call on your life and respond quicker than I have. Your calling could be a Bible teacher, a missionary, a pastor or it could also be making phone calls to those who are lost, writing notes to people who are sick or just spending time in prayer for your church several times throughout the day. Whatever it is, don't trivialize it, don't make excuses and follow the Holy Spirit as He brings you to a place where there is such peace and joy that you can't experience it until you let God work mightily in your life.

When I started writing this book, Jeff was coming up on seven months in the hospital but as I closed the book he had already gone on to be with the Lord. He never got well enough to go to a nursing home and had very few good days among the bad. Jeff, throughout his illness, was never ready to let go and the doctors always did their best to keep him here. Before I left Jeff for my last vacation we read the scripture about being content in all circumstances, and Jeff admitted that this was getting really hard for him to do. He would have never admitted this before because always in the past he continued to believe he was going to be totally healed, that he would be normal again but I believe that was the moment he began to understand what his body was going through. Please pray for my family as we go through this loss and that we will have peace and know God's perfect will for our lives.

So, what do you do, when your nickname's Job? You have faith. You receive God's grace. You must not ever turn away but make the choice to tackle every challenge with God's strength. When you are discouraged or are questioning your circumstances, please remember the perseverance of Job. He loved the Lord through it all, and was upright, and righteous in all he did. No suffering is too great to turn our backs on our Savior. Faithfulness is what you need.

Thank you for your time and God Bless You!

> Lord, I just want to thank you again for giving me this opportunity. I pray that what I have shared here will help someone in their walk with you. Thanks, again, for caring for me and guiding me to this point. I love you so. In Jesus' name. Amen.